CW00339814

Healing in his Wings

Healing in his Wings

Memoirs of a Flight Medical Officer

Air Commodore Iain McCoubrey

[signature]

24 ii 22

The Book Guild Ltd

First published in Great Britain in 2019 by
The Book Guild Ltd
9 Priory Business Park
Wistow Road, Kibworth
Leicestershire, LE8 0RX
Freephone: 0800 999 2982
www.bookguild.co.uk
Email: info@bookguild.co.uk
Twitter: @bookguild

Copyright © 2019 Iain McCoubrey

The right of Iain McCoubrey to be identified as the author of this
work has been asserted by him in accordance with the
Copyright, Design and Patents Act 1988.

All rights reserved. No part of this publication may be
reproduced, transmitted, or stored in a retrieval system, in any form or by any means,
without permission in writing from the publisher, nor be otherwise circulated in
any form of binding or cover other than that in which it is published and without
a similar condition being imposed on the subsequent purchaser.

Typeset in Adobe Garamond Pro

Printed and bound in the UK by TJ International, Padstow, Cornwall

ISBN 978 1912881 017

British Library Cataloguing in Publication Data.
A catalogue record for this book is available from the British Library.

In Memoriam
John Garnons Williams
1946–2007

Contents

Introduction

I have always been excited by flying. An early photograph shows me sitting in an aeroplane on a children's roundabout at a funfair in Ayr in 1948. I am told it was my favourite ride. At my first school the best game was "Spitfire Pilots" – you put your school cap on back to front, extended your arms and ran along the school wall making a noise supposedly like that of a Merlin engine. My prep school library had all the *Biggles* books and I read the lot at least once. At school I joined the RAF section of the Combined Cadet Force, learned to glide, and won a flying scholarship which provided me with enough flying to qualify for a private pilot's licence. As a medical student I joined the University Air Squadron, gaining my Preliminary Flying Badge – the so called "Budgie Wings" – and being commissioned into the RAF Medical Branch as a Cadet in 1967.

During my flying scholarship training I had a mild medical problem, so in the summer between A levels and university I was sent to the RAF Hospital at Wroughton in Wiltshire for investigations. The problem (hyperventilation) was quickly identified and dealt with but it triggered in me a fascination with Aviation Medicine. It was a surprise to no one when I decided upon a medical career in the Royal Air Force.

I served from 1967 to 1997. When I joined we still had a number of people serving who had fought in WWII. When I left, the cold war was over, cuts and downsizing were epidemic, overseas posts were disappearing and GPS was making navigation too easy. Despite – or perhaps because of – the existential threats we faced there was a great spirit of camaraderie and *joie de vivre* throughout my time in the service. Political correctness and 'elfnsafety' did not dominate the scene – although *flight* safety always did. Time has moved on. The Royal Air Force still defends the nation and offers great opportunities for those serving in it. But the air force I joined no longer exists.

I always said that I would remain in the Royal Air Force "as long as I was having fun". One day I realised that I wasn't having fun any more. So I left. This book is about the memorable and amusing bits of my service. The humdrum and routine has, I hope, been omitted.

Throughout, I have described myself as a "medical officer" – that is, an RAF officer whose specialty is medicine. I saw that as being quite different to being "a doctor in the air force". A Flight Medical Officer, to quote the official publication, is one who "has obtained the Diploma in Aviation Medicine and has successfully completed the Royal Air Force's complementary Flight Medical Officer's course."

1

In The Beginning

I was commissioned as a Pilot Officer in the Royal Air Force Medical Branch on the 24th of July 1967. As a medical student, the biggest difference I noticed was the money. I was paid about nine-tenths of what a pre-registration house officer was paid. Compared with my fellow students I was rich; and I made the most of it.

My medical studies continued as before. I had already been flying in the University Air Squadron for three years. Landing my Chipmunk aircraft amid the various commercial airliners at Glasgow Airport almost convinced me that I was a real pilot. Thanks to the Nelsonian eyes of two of my Squadron commanders, Wing Commander John Greenhill and Squadron Leader Barry Dale, I was able to continue flying as a result of a tortuous (and obviously incorrect, as the powers that be made clear when they rumbled it) misinterpretation of the rules about people like me continuing to receive flying training. During my undergraduate years I amassed just over 200 flying hours on the Chipmunk.

Fitting in flying with the demands placed on a senior medical student was not easy; but help was regularly at hand. When six of us turned up for our attachment to an ophthalmology clinic, the consultant, in his introductory talk, said that "statistically, none of you is going to become an ophthalmologist. You are most welcome here, but I am not noting attendance". Much of my "Eyes" time was spent flying. On one occasion, when the weather was too bad and I did turn up, there were five of us at the clinic. The understanding consultant greeted us with, "Five today – are there no good films on?"

In the midst of all the bumph I had received on appointment as a medical cadet was expressed a hope that cadets might spend some vacation time in an RAF hospital to further their experience of the service. In 1967 Prime Minister Harold Wilson had announced that British Forces would be withdrawn from East of Suez by the end of the decade; I was due to graduate in July 1970. So, very much tongue in cheek, I wrote to my headquarters and said I would be delighted to spend some time in an RAF hospital, and what about the one at Changi, in Singapore?

Rather to my surprise, they agreed to my spending three weeks at Changi. Back then we didn't travel as much as we do now, and a chance to go to the Far East was very exciting. I had to get kitted out with tropical uniform and organise a number of inoculations. When I got there, the humid Singapore heat, the noise, the bustle, the sights and especially the smell was unlike anything I'd experienced before. Changi was then still relatively undeveloped and the food stalls in Changi village, with the various family-run shops catering to the service population with camera dealers, porcelain sellers and tailors, truly felt exotic. And I was able to see the infamous Changi Jail, where the Japanese had abused so many prisoners during WWII. At that time it was being used to house those who had displeased Lee Kuan Yu, Singapore's strong man in the lead up to independence.

In theory I was to be working with the anaesthetics department at the hospital. I had spent the previous summer as an "extern" (like an intern, but from outside the system) in the department of anaesthesiology of the University of Tennessee in Memphis, and had found the specialty interesting. In practice I spent a lot of my time trying to arrange to go flying. I managed flights in a Meteor target towing aircraft (quite exciting, and not as dangerous as it sounds), a Single Pioneer investigating possible sites of remnants of the communist insurgency in Malaysia and a Shackleton maritime patrol aircraft (very boring, but the scenery was great). The senior consultant anaesthetist at Changi was very understanding about my frequent absences. I was able to repay the favour some years later when his son applied to join the RAF medical branch and I could support his application. And of course I returned home with a rather fine suit from Thai Singh tailors.

Back at home, it was soon time for Finals, then my two six-month house jobs – one in medicine and one in surgery. I then went on leave to get married. My long-suffering wife Vivien, after some years as my long-suffering girlfriend, had dealt with my enthusiasm for flying on the basis of "If you can't beat 'em, join 'em". She won a short service commission in the WRAF and served until we were married. I suspect it wasn't her first choice of job after graduating, but it exemplifies the rock-solid support she gave me throughout our life together in the RAF.

We honeymooned on the west coast of Ireland – presciently, for we loved the country but because of "the Troubles" I would be prohibited from visiting it for the rest of my service. I then reported to the Officer Cadet Training Unit at RAF Henlow to begin my initial officer training. The first thing they did was to despatch us to Henlow town to buy a hat, so that we could doff it either to "salute" or in response to a salute. The men's outfitters were ready for us. I suspect the various courses passing through kept the business going.

When you have spent the previous year working very hard and making life or death decisions, marching and drill are marvellous relaxations. You quite literally don't have to think which way to turn. Our course included a psychiatrist, a vicar and an Australian moving from the Royal Australian Air Force to the RAF. We did our best, but struggled to take it as seriously as our instructor. Because we were all commissioned officers – as opposed to officer cadets –

we were drilled by the Senior Warrant Officer, a fierce and skeletal man with a loud voice and a big stick, known as The Screaming Skull. (His office, of course, was known as Golgotha.) I suspect he had few expectations of such a motley crew. He was right.

There followed leadership training as well as instruction in the organisation of and administration in the RAF and its medical services; and of course more aviation medicine. In the last week of training my career nearly came to an abrupt end. I returned to the museum at the RAF Institute of Pathology after a good lunch, and saw at the far end my colleague Mike Gibson bent over an exhibit, with his backside sticking out. I ran towards him preparing to deliver a sharp kick. As I got to within two yards, he stood up and I realised that actually it wasn't Mike, but rather Air Vice Marshal Paddy Griffin, the RAF's chief orthopaedic surgeon, who was due to lecture to us. I managed to stop; I tried to look composed; but the Air Marshal's look told me he thought I was a very odd character indeed.

Then it was off to work for real. My first posting was as a junior medical officer at the Royal Air Force College at Cranwell. This pleased me greatly, as it was from there that I had taken off on my first solo flight while at University Air Squadron Summer Camp in 1965.

Cranwell was in the middle of significant change. Since its foundation in 1919 it had taken young men straight from school as Flight Cadets and over three years given them a tertiary-level education in science and the humanities, while training them to fly and become RAF officers. In the early 1970s this didn't fit with what the educational establishment wanted. The new way was to take young men and now women from University, and give them a shorter course concentrating solely on RAF matters. When I arrived, the last Flight Cadet entry was reaching its end. The first Graduate Entry courses were making their way through. Having HRH The Prince of Wales as a member of No 1 Graduate Entry Course helped lubricate the change, but there were still a lot of teething problems during the changeover; not least that occasionally an ex Flight Cadet flying instructor would be junior in rank to his Graduate Entry student.

There were still a number of personnel on the station who had fought in WWII. The College Commandant, Air Vice Marshal Desmond Hughes, had been a Battle of Britain pilot. The one-eyed station commander, Group Captain Gerald Pendred, told stories of advancing across Europe after D-Day from one captured German base to another in his Spitfire. Perhaps most interestingly, in the Station Dental Centre there was an elderly corporal dental hygienist, who wore pilot's wings and had a chestful of medals. He had been a sergeant pilot in Bomber Command during the war and was occasionally heard to mutter that he had a greater right to wear his wings than some of the young men whose teeth he scraped and polished.

Although the social changes associated with "the sixties" were percolating through all three services, within the RAF, Cranwell, unsurprisingly, kept the old ways going for longest. When I carried out home visits to patients in senior officers' married quarters, it was expected that I would take my gloves. (At the commandant's house, the steward took your gloves and hat on arrival and returned them as you left.) "Calling" and the dropping off of cards had just been done away with (my informal welcoming letter told me that "cards were no longer required"); but the station commander's wife was still "At Home" one afternoon a week, and newly arrived wives were expected to call on her as soon as possible. Vivien was expected to join the rota to arrange flowers in the Officers' Mess. But there was also a lot of support. Vivien was taken under the wing of a very senior officer's wife, who in a helpful and totally unpatronising way, guided her through the various hazards faced by a new officer's wife (in all senses of that phrase).

My Senior Medical Officer (SMO), Group Captain David Hills, was very supportive of what must have been a rather Tiggerish new arrival. He arranged for me to be trained so as to deputise for the Medical Officer Pilot in lecturing to students on aviation medicine and conducting hypoxia (lack of oxygen) training in the decompression chamber. I became unofficial medical adviser to the college aerobatic display team, the Poachers, preparing a small pack with various medications to take with them on tour. It caused much ribald comment on one occasion when I labelled a broad-spectrum antibiotic as being "for *nasty* infections". Cautiously, I began to feel my way in general practice, with David Hills as an excellent trainer.

My past kept up with me. On one occasion I was called to the airfield to meet an aircraft which had suffered fumes in its cockpit. The routine was to check over the crew, and take blood samples to look for any adverse effects. The aircraft captain was Flight Lieutenant Mike Brooke, a former instructor in my University Air Squadron. He was amused but anxious as one of his former students stuck a needle into his arm. When I declared him fit, he wasn't sure he wanted to believe that either.

As was the custom in those days, after a year or so to settle down in the service, new medical officers tended to be posted overseas. There was little attempt to deny the belief that this was a cynical move by the personnel staff to convince you that RAF life was wonderful, and that as a result you would sign up for a permanent commission. So it was that in December 1972 Vivien and I set out with almost all our belongings in our car for RAF Bruggen, on the Dutch/German border in Germany.

Bruggen was very different from Cranwell. It was, as Group Captain Peter Harding, the station commander, regularly said, the "steel tip of the sharp end" of the RAF. (Some years later, and as a Marshal of the Royal Air Force, he hit the headlines of the *News of the World* and resigned as Chief of Defence Staff over his affair with Lady Bienvenida Buck, wife of a Conservative MP). The three flying squadrons had just been equipped with Phantom FGR2 strike/attack aircraft and the pick of RAF aircrew had been assigned to them. The station was defended by a squadron of Bloodhound surface-to-air missiles. We exercised in preparation for WWIII all the time. There was an annual Tactical Evaluation (Taceval) by NATO staff; in preparation for this the station commander would call a "minival" about once a month, with alert horns and hooters going off all over the station in the middle of the night and everyone rushing to their place of duty so as to be able to report that we were manned to the minimum requirement within the prescribed time. For much of the time during exercises we had to work in Nuclear, Biological and Chemical (NBC) protective clothing and gas masks and had to work within sealed areas with airlocks if we wanted to take them off. When a minival or Taceval was taking place, all medical care other than for emergencies was stopped. After the exercise was over, everyone else went home or to the mess to relax and have a drink. By contrast, the medical officers found themselves overwhelmed with patients who had not been able to access medical care for the past 24–36 hours, and now insisted on doing so. We found this very irritating

The recent expansion at Bruggen meant that there wasn't enough accommodation at the station for everyone to be housed locally. When we first moved to Germany, we lived in a pokey second-floor flat above a chip shop some 10 miles (or 16 kilometres, as I should probably say) away from the station. We were lucky. Some of the junior non-commissioned men found themselves living in what looked like converted hen-houses over the border in Holland, with the landlord making advances to the young wife while the husband was away sometimes for several days. It made for a lot of stress, which resulted in increased workload for the medical centre.

I was appointed squadron medical officer to 14 Squadron, the first of the Phantom squadrons to be formed and in their (probably correct) estimation, the best. They were a hard bunch. Successful military aircrew tend to have a particular type of personality. The best were stable extroverts. Some, perhaps better for battle but not so easy to live with otherwise, tended towards the seriously aggressive. If I were to give them the best support, I had to gain their confidence. While this was sometimes hard work, it was also great fun – although occasionally I felt that my liver didn't agree.

The SMO when I arrived at Bruggen, Wing Commander Alan Johnston, had come to us from the RAF Institute of Aviation Medicine at Farnborough. His breadth of knowledge was very helpful to me as I learned about it all on the job. The realisation that your war role was actually to get the maximum number of sorties out of a limited number of aircrew by whatever means was a bit of an eye-opener to this enthusiastic and naïve twenty-six-year-old. Sadly, we had a number of fatal aircraft accidents during my time at Bruggen. Alan's explanation and advice on how a medical officer should deal with both the accident investigation and the aftermath were invaluable.

I was appointed editor of the station magazine – the *Bruggen Circuit*. As well as printing news about all the station's squadrons and their personnel, it carried items of "general interest". I wrote the horoscope. This filled a whole page in the magazine and was enormously popular with the readers. I made the whole thing up, so it was (as indeed is all astrology) complete poppycock, but I regularly would have someone telling me how accurate it was and trying to seek out the author for a personal consultation. On the inside back page was the "Bruggenbird of the Month". It wasn't quite *Country Life*'s "girl with pearls", but neither was it anywhere near the *Sun*'s page 3; and of course you couldn't have anything like it today. I never had any difficulty finding volunteers. One of the most memorable pictures, to me at any rate, was of my SMO Alan Johnston's teenage daughter Bridget, who was very easy on the eyes anyway, skiing in a bikini. Alan offered it to me and said, "What do you think of that?" Given that he was (a) her father and (b) my boss, I had to temper my thoughts a little before replying.

Aircrew were trained to cope with crashing or being shot down in a cold environment at the RAF Winter Survival School in Bad Kohlgrub (inevitably known as Cold Badgrub) in Bavaria. As well as being taught survival skills, students did a fair bit of skiing to promote fitness, and various practical exercises. The whole thing finished off with an escape-and-evasion exercise. Over three days students practised building shelters and getting food, keeping warm, and then finally making a cross-country break to a supposed safe haven. This last took place overnight, and students were pursued by German ski troops. Very few ever made it. If you were caught, your resistance to interrogation was put to the test by "tactical questioning". Details of this remain classified, but in general terms they were quite sharp and didn't always remember to say please and thank you. It had to be supervised by, inter alia, a medical officer who had been through the process himself. (No, I don't know what they did on the first course). To that end I found myself in Bavaria in January 1974 and cold, wet and hungry was caught by the ski troops. A tradition had grown up that, when they captured you, the Germans (who had seen the same war films as we had), would say, "Zo, Englander, for you ze war is over." I would have to say that it didn't seem particularly funny at that precise moment. The experience in the next few hours, if not exactly enjoyable, offered me an insight into myself I probably wouldn't have had otherwise.

When I returned to oversee a later exercise, I was offered a lift down to Bavaria in the official aircraft of the Air Officer Commanding (AOC) the RAF in Germany, Air Vice Marshal Philip Lagesen. He, together with the RAF's chief doctor in Germany, Air Commodore Wyn Perkins, was going down on a familiarisation visit. I had been told to report to the airfield at 0830; as a keen young officer I was there at 0815. This was just as well, as I had been given the wrong time. Departure had been set for 0800 and the aircraft was sitting on the tarmac with the engines running and a couple of very cross Air Officers inside. I was hurried on board and off we went to a Luftwaffe base outside Munich. From there a helicopter was to take us to Bad Kohlgrub.

It was Rosenmontag – the climax of the German carnival season – and we had expected the base to be quiet. It was very quiet. No one met the aircraft and there was no sign of a helicopter. The AOC became even less happy. His ADC was sent to try to find someone. The ADC didn't speak any German; but I did, having been sent on an excellent German language course by the RAF, so I went with him. Eventually we found someone who could help and, after about a quarter of an hour, a helicopter appeared. We all got in, the helicopter took off, and the pilot turned to us.

"Where to?"

"RAF Winter Survival School."

"Where's that?"

"Bad Kohlgrub."

"Where's that?"

Cue further furrows on the AOC's brow. It quickly transpired that I was the only one on board who knew where our destination was, so I sat up front with a map and directed the pilot. Wyn Perkins was very pleased to have one of his medical officers save the day, and assured me that I had made complete expiation for turning up late.

Aircrew spent some time each year at an armament practice camp at an Italian Air Force Base near Decimomannu in Sardinia. I contrived a visit to 14 Squadron when they were there and managed to get one of the only two flights I had in a Phantom. "Deci" was a tri-service base with RAF, Luftwaffe and Italian Air Force personnel present. A number of surely apocryphal stories circulated about discussions late at night in the mess. My favourite two both concern German reactions to a particularly voluble and boastful Italian pilot holding forth about his derring-do. In one, the German turns to the Brit, groans, and says, "Just remember, next war it's your turn to have them." In the other, the German stands up, pokes the Italian in the chest and says, "Shut up. At least in the last war we came second."

Although I was learning more about general practice and aviation medicine, the steepest learning curve I had was in paediatrics. Vivien spent half of our three years in Germany pregnant. When we were living above the chip shop, it had taken me some time to realise that the reason for Vivien feeling sick most mornings was not in fact the smell of frying wafting in through the window. Our daughter Clare was born in 1973 and our son Robin in 1975. Both were registered with the British Consulate in Dusseldorf within two weeks of birth so as to ensure not only that they *were* British, but also that they were exempt from German military service. Having two children under two away from the support of our families was hard work – especially for Vivien – but we had some wonderful family holidays caravanning around Europe.

During my time in Germany I had been granted a permanent commission (yes, the bribe worked) and I needed to make plans for my future career. I wanted to be an SMO on a flying station. I would be best prepared for this by gaining the Diploma in Aviation Medicine. The RAF Institute of Aviation Medicine (IAM) at Farnborough ran a six-month course to train for the diploma and I applied to attend it on my return to UK. To my great delight I was selected. I was about to sit the Membership examination of the Royal College of General Practitioners, so an academic few months were in store. The caravan we'd had our European holidays in now became my study and I would decamp to the station caravan park where I could immerse myself in my books without the interruptions of two small children. I sat the MRCGP exam in December 1975 just before heading home for Farnborough and the IAM.

2

Ut Secure Volent

Ut Secure Volent – That They May Fly Safely – was the motto of the Royal Air Force Institute of Aviation Medicine. Based at Farnborough, within the grounds of the Royal Aircraft Establishment, it had been founded in 1945 as the successor to the wartime RAF Physiological Laboratory. Originally led by Professor Sir Bryan Matthews CBE FRS, subsequently professor of physiology at Cambridge, it was by the 1970s a world leader in aviation medicine research.

The need for aviation medicine training for RAF medical officers other than the research physiologists who worked at the Institute had been addressed by means of a variety of courses over the years. In the mid 1960s, things were regularised by the setting up of a Diploma in Aviation Medicine (DAvMed), awarded under the aegis of the Royal College of Physicians of London, with an academically rigorous six-month course to prepare students for the Diploma exam, run by IAM.

We left Bruggen in December 1975, and spent Christmas with my parents in Scotland before I reported to Farnborough in January 1976. We had arrived at my parents' house late in the day, and the children were tired and needed to be fed, bathed and put to bed in short order. I was aware that my father was hovering in a way that suggested he had something to say, but it wasn't until the children were settled that he came to the point. Had I passed the MRCGP exam? I had, to my great relief, but my somewhat chequered career as an undergraduate (in no way related to absenting myself to go flying, you must understand) meant that he had been more worried about the result than I was. I think it was almost as good a Christmas present for him as it was for me.

The Commandant of IAM at the time was Group Captain Peter Howard. He had been awarded an OBE for his work on the physiological aspects of developing the rocket-propelled ejection seat; and then putting his money where his mouth was by becoming the first person to eject using one as part of the testing process.

There were some interesting characters on the research staff. Group Captain John Ernsting was a magnificent caricature of "the absent-minded professor" with his unruly wavy hair and a constant air of his mind still being back in the laboratory. Group Captain Tom Whiteside came from Glasgow, and despite his years in Hampshire still had a noticeable "Kelvinside" accent. But he had a French wife, and was qualified as a Grade I MoD interpreter in that language. Watching him interpret at international conferences was astonishing. The cautious, gently spoken west of Scotland academic, when he switched to French mode had, as well as a perfect accent, the body language, hunched shoulders, pouted lips and strange "Hein?" noises of a Parisian native.

The DAvMed course was internationally renowned. My fellow students were three other RAF medical officers, with two from the Royal Navy and one from the RAMC. There were three Canadian civilians, a Royal Australian Air Force Group Captain, a Major from the Thai Air Force, a Captain from the Egyptian Air Force, a Captain from the Kenyan Air Force and a Malaysian Sikh Major from the Royal Malaysian Air Force. Mixed bunch though we were, we soon became a mutually supportive and lively group.

Homo sapiens has evolved to live at ground level, travel no faster that he can propel himself and survive the normal effects of gravity.

Flying takes him higher, to colder atmospheres with less pressure and less oxygen. Higher speed of itself is no problem, but getting to it and manoeuvring during it produce significant problems due to acceleration. At increased speed and height and with reduced oxygen supply, our special senses (vision, hearing and the like) are more likely to get confused. It was so that we could understand and manage or prevent these problems, as well as looking at the effects of illness on fitness to fly, that we had a six-month programme of lectures, demonstrations, experiments and experiences.

We settled into formal lectures fairly quickly; but after not very long the undergraduates who had been dormant within our mature personae began to reappear. The lecture room at IAM was very well equipped, with almost everything in the room (blinds, lights, etc.) being controllable from the desk. The single exception was the fluorescent light over the blackboard. A favourite trick was to let a guest lecturer (never the IAM staff; they would have recognised it for what it was) write a few things on the board, then for me, sitting at the back, to raise my hand and say, "Excuse me sir, I can't quite read the board. Would you switch the light on please?" About fifty per cent of the time the lecturer would study the control panel and with a bit of luck would press some buttons causing blinds to go up and down and lights to go on and off. When this had gone on for just enough time, Major Sagoo, our Malaysian Sikh, would rise from his seat at the front row, glare at the lecturer as his ancestors might well have done down their *jezzails* in the Khyber pass, switch on the light, glare again, and sit down without a word. It usually took the lecturer several minutes to recover. More confident lecturers merely said, "Where's the switch?"

An even better wheeze, when the lecturer appeared seriously under-confident, was to swap seats when the lecturer's back was turned. Very childish, but great fun; and however bewildered they looked, no one ever challenged us.

On Wednesdays in most weeks we would visit a laboratory, training facility, factory or similar establishment elsewhere. We travelled in an old and rather basic RAF coach. However there was plenty of space, and once we had appointed one of our number as wines officer, we had a regular source of refreshment installed at the back. It greatly brightened up return journeys.

We visited the prototype Concorde, then undergoing testing at RAF Fairford. Although the reason for the visit was to look at the special oxygen system installed to protect the pilots in the event of a loss of cabin pressure at very high altitude, we had been promised that, if the timing of a test flight suited, we would be allowed to fly in her. Sadly, she had returned a day late from her cold weather trials in Canada, and so we missed out on the chance of a flight. I never did fly in Concorde. Many years later, when I was living in Oxfordshire, I would hear her flying over the village while in church on a Sunday morning. On one memorable occasion the vicar was running a bit late, and during the Second Collect, for Peace, he had just said the words "O Lord, author of peace and lover of concord" when she flew over with her unmistakeable roar. Wonderful.

We studied the practical aspects of survival after ejection, crashing or being shot down and finishing up in the sea in a number of ways. At the Sea Survival School on the South Coast we bobbed about the Channel in both single-man dinghies (very difficult to climb into from the sea) and multi-person dinghies (stabler but very sea-sick-making) in the middle of a snowstorm. Poor Major Htue, from Thailand, who was as thin as a rake and not used to such weather, clearly suffered most despite us all wearing the best protective clothing. A tot of rum on the safety boat after we were picked up was most welcome.

Another immersion in water took place at the Royal Navy's "Dunker" trainer in Portsmouth. It was used to train helicopter aircrew in case of ditching. A helicopter fuselage was suspended in a frame above a deep water tank, then dropped into the water. Sometimes it settled in an upright position, and sometimes it rolled over and settled upside down. The crew (us) were strapped inside the fuselage and had to get out; but only once the fuselage had stopped moving. We received a full briefing, including advice that you shouldn't take a deep breath and start holding it until the water was up to your shoulders. Somewhat anxious, in we went. The fuselage started to roll upside down. It settled in the water and I concentrated on getting everything absolutely right, especially waiting to take a deep breath until the water reached my shoulders. As it advanced from my scalp towards my eyebrows, I realised that the advice only applied when entering the water upright. Fortunately, I managed a quick breath just in time.

There were of course safety personnel; two divers with scuba apparatus were in the tank and a free swimmer, in swimming trunks but with a knife to cut harnesses in case of problems, was in the fuselage itself. We did three "drops". After the first drop, and particularly when we noticed that the free swimmer was able to remain seated in the fuselage until it was pulled free of the water again, we relaxed and enjoyed it rather more.

The course dealt with all aspects of aviation medicine, both military and civil. We spent a week at British Airways' (BA) training centre at Heathrow learning about their particular challenges. The climax of the week was lunch on the Friday, served to us in a mock-up first-class cabin by stewardesses under training. The lunch was excellent – as well it might be for BA's first-class passengers. The service was excellent too, with the stewardesses doing their best to impress both trainers and "customers". As we had been warned, at the end of lunch there was a simulated aircraft fire, and the cabin filled with harmless but impenetrable white smoke, as a result of which you quite literally couldn't see your hand in front of you. The stewardesses had to guide us through the smoke out of the cabin to the escape chute. I shan't go into details, but I will leave you to imagine the goings-on when a number of young doctors who have enjoyed BA's excellent wine are manhandled out of an aircraft cabin by roughly the same number of high-spirited stewardesses. The subsequent slide down the escape chute was merely the icing on the cake.

Another visit had a less happy outcome. We were at The Martin Baker Aircraft Company, who make the ejection seats which have saved many aircrew lives. Halfway through the morning a message reached me from Farnborough that my father was very seriously ill. He had had heart problems for many years, but when we had spoken on the phone the previous Saturday he had been well. I asked the Martin Baker manager who was showing us round if he could arrange for me to have a lift to the nearest station, so that I could make my way home then head for Scotland. He would have none of it, but instead insisted on having me driven all the way back to Farnborough. Vivien took me to Heathrow, I flew up to Edinburgh and was able to visit my father in hospital in the Borders that evening. My mother, sister and I had a gentle chat with him, and when he got tired and fell asleep, we left him. He died that night. I have always had a high opinion of Martin Baker and their products, but their kindness that day puts them in a special place for me.

My father's funeral was held two days later, in the village church where he had been an Elder. We drove down to the village about five minutes before the service was due to begin, to find the centre of the village crowded with cars, and no parking available anywhere. A policeman was directing traffic. I drove up to him, explained who I was, and asked for some help.

"Leave your car here, Sir. It'll be fine. And I'm sorry about your father – he was a great man."

I thought so too, and I knew he was popular, but this took me by surprise. Inside the church it was standing room only (though they had kept seats for us). After the service as we headed out of the village towards the crematorium, there were more policemen about and it became apparent that they had effectively closed down the village except for those attending the funeral. The sense of a whole community mourning was very moving and I drove on with some difficulty. A few weeks later I had the most extraordinary and vivid dream of my life. In it I was sitting with my father in the little living room beside the kitchen in my family home, and I was telling him all about the funeral. He was as astonished as I had been. As it took place, I knew that it had to be a dream; but it felt more real than anything I have experienced before or since.

On Monday I was back in Farnborough. I received the most gentle of tickings-off for technically being Absent Without Leave and was given a post-dated leave form to complete; then it was back to work.

As the DAvMed exam approached, we were given subjects on which we had to prepare a revision lecture for our colleagues. Being the youngest, I was given "The Effects of Ageing in Aviation". When we got to the exam and looked at the paper, one of the questions (it was in the days of "answer any five of eight questions") was "Discuss the effects of ageing in aviation". During the post exam panic and discussions, my colleagues expressed some chagrin that "my" subject had come up in the exam. They assumed it had given me an unfair advantage. When I admitted that actually I hadn't answered that question because, unlike them, I was aware of all that my presentation *hadn't* covered, there were some sharp intakes of breath.

Despite that, we all passed the exam – the first course to have a 100% pass rate. Captain Faisal Fawzi from Egypt was the first person from his country to have gained the DAvMed, and was sufficiently surprised that he twice left the pub where we were all celebrating to go back to the examination hall to recheck the results.

As I've said above, I didn't always cover myself with academic glory at university. But in aviation medicine I found a subject which really "got" me, and probably as a result my performance improved. I came top in the exam and was awarded the Stewart Memorial Prize – named for Air Vice Marshal Bill Stewart, the first commandant of the IAM and like me another medical graduate of the University of Glasgow. The overseas students departed, and the British forces medical officers began the one-month Flight

Medical Officers' course, where the theory taught for the DAvMed was dovetailed into the practice of the RAF, Navy and Army. We all got our end-of-course postings. I was to go as SMO to RAF Valley, in Anglesey. It was exactly what I wanted.

3

Iechyd Da

People used to say that serving at RAF Valley should be counted as an overseas tour: it was a long way away, you had to cross the sea to get there, and the locals spoke a different language.

At the end of the Flight Medical Officers' course I had been promoted and was now a Squadron Leader. I had been awarded the Flight Medical Officers' flying badge on the strength of my University Air Squadron flying. With that and my recent medical qualifications I felt that I was fully prepared for my new job.

Anglesey was certainly a long way from Farnborough. The incumbent SMO, Wing Commander John Baird, was due to leave before my arrival, and we were both keen on an in-depth handover; the locum MO who would be there between us would be unable to give me nearly as much information. I negotiated a couple of days off and planned my drive to Valley. Looking at the road map, I assumed it would take me four to five hours. John assured me that it would be much nearer eight. He was right. In 1976 the A5 was not a fast road, and I seemed to drive through every single town and village between Shrewsbury and Anglesey. It was a bit of a flog, but worth it for the handover.

When the time came to move, I went on ahead of the family, taking my motorbike with me on the train to Holyhead. I had never got into motorbikes in my youth. A neighbour at Bruggen had let me try his, and I was won over. I had bought myself a motorbike as a reward for passing the MRCGP; and justified it by telling myself it would be very useful for going to and from work at Farnborough. After about six months at Valley, and having seen far too many horrendous outcomes of motorbike accidents, I sold it and have never ridden one since.

I took over our married quarter the next morning and waited for Vivien's arrival with the children at the end of the day. Taking two young children on an eight-hour drive along winding roads is never much fun. We had bought a stick-on toy steering wheel for Clare, who was therefore able to help with the driving. In order to avoid some of the "Are we there yet?" demands, the children had been told that they wouldn't have reached Wales until they crossed the Menai Bridge. Clare caused an outbreak of laughter at the Little Chef (remember them?) in Llangollen when she announced to the world at large that "we are going to Wales".

The next morning I returned to Farnborough to hand back our married quarter there. Taking over and handing over a married quarter, known as "marching in" and "marching out", involved a detailed inventory of everything in it as well as a thorough inspection to ensure absolute cleanliness. It was a complete pain. I had no sooner left Valley than Vivien started to feel unwell and by the end of the day was vomiting regularly and profusely. It really isn't how one wants to make one's entrance as the new SMO's wife, but finally Vivien felt she had to phone the medical centre and ask for help. The locum SMO, Squadron Leader Warwick Pike, came round on a home visit. Seeing the state Vivien was in, he gave her an intravenous injection of a strong anti-vomiting drug, and advised her to lie down. It shows quite how ill she was that she did so without asking questions or thinking about anything else.

At sometime in the early morning the next day she awoke, feeling rather better, and remembered that she had two children. She got up, looked round the house and found them asleep in their beds. When they woke up, they told Mummy how the nice doctor had made them some supper, given them a bath and put them to bed. Warwick Pike, whom we scarcely knew at the time, became a close friend and colleague over the next twenty years or so. But his noble acts on that day – above and beyond the call of duty – made him a family hero.

Although not the steel tip of the sharp end that Bruggen was, RAF Valley was a very dynamic station. No 4 Flying Training School had four squadrons, three flying the Folland Gnat and one the Hawker Hunter. They were replaced by Hawk trainers midway through my tour. There was the Strike Command Air-to-Air Missile Establishment, which hosted fighters coming to practise firing their missiles on the range at Aberporth a few miles south of us. The Search and Rescue Helicopter Training Unit was at Valley, as well as "C" Flight 22 Squadron, providing operational search and rescue (SAR) Wessex helicopters. The station was a Master Diversion Airfield, which meant it was open twenty-four hours a day every day of the year as a possible landing place for aircraft who couldn't get in elsewhere – usually because of the weather.

The Station Medical Centre was a fairly modern building, situated outside the perimeter wire, between the station and the married quarters. My window looked across a green sward towards the lake which lay in front of the officers' mess. The green sward was ideal for SAR helicopters either to land patients at the medical centre or pick me up if I went off on a job with them. When the water in the lake was low you could just see the wheels of an upturned car. Apparently many years previously, the lake had frozen solid and a car had been driven on to it. For whatever reason, its owner left it there overnight. During the night it thawed. The car is still there.

Kipling said that, "The backbone of the Army is the non-commissioned man." I'm sure he would have included the RAF, but when he wrote the poem in the 1890s there wasn't one. My Flight Sergeant, Barry Hodgson, was an exemplar of all one could hope for and gave me outstanding support in my first tour as an SMO. He had contacts throughout the station and could solve any problem. I must have sung his praises at home in the children's hearing as they were totally overawed on first meeting him. As Clare explained to her little brother, "Daddy is a doctor but Mr Hodgson runs the medical centre."

One of the flying training school squadrons invited me to be an honorary member, and thanks to the encouragement and support of the SAR flight commander, Flight Lieutenant John Garnons Williams, I had plenty of opportunity to go flying. John and his wife Kate had two children the same ages as ours and we had a lot else in common; we became lifelong friends. As well as being able to see the aircrew at work in their "office" and therefore better understand any problems they might have, flying with them helps to build up a rapport and gain some credibility and trust. This matters, because it is all too easy for the MO to be seen as a person who exists solely to ground people for some medical reason which seems to the sufferer to be completely irrelevant and for them therefore to put off consulting him when they would probably be better to do so.

I did a dozen or so SAR jobs at Valley. One of the first things I learned about such sorties is that the information you receive over the radio about the casualty is likely to be unreliable. My first job was to recover a seaman, who had been "electrocuted", from a Liverpool pilot boat. On the way out I worried about how long he might have been pulseless and how my resuscitation technique would work on board a relatively small vessel. When we got there he was standing on deck waiting for us. We transported him to a hospital ashore, in very good health.

Once we were called to pick up a seaman with a head injury from a Russian intelligence-gathering vessel, one of which was often at sea on our extended runway centre line. This caused a little consternation on the station. Should we go? Was it a trap? As soon as we stepped aboard we would be seized and it would be "next stop Vladivostok"? Appropriate opinions were sought and off we went. We were lowered on board, and I took the winchman with me to watch my back. As we were guided into the bowels of the ship, I saw lots of posters, which seemed vaguely familiar, but not quite right. Then it struck me. Just as we had recognition posters for Russian aircraft, so they had posters for ours; and that was what I was looking at. The casualty had a cut on his temple, but it was well bandaged. We took him off, but when I attempted to engage him in conversation all I got was "Nyet". I had thought to take him to my medical centre, examine and if necessary further treat the cut, then return him. But I was young, naive, and thinking "doctor". The station commander, whose voice was instantly recognisable on the radio, made it clear that he was not allowed anywhere near RAF Valley. We took him to the hospital in Bangor, where I briefed the junior doctor to whom I handed him over that the patient was a Russian who, if not thoroughly investigated and fully treated, might be the cause of an international incident. She took the bait and it was three days until he was eventually returned by boat to the Russian vessel. During that time it was stuck in our bit of the Irish Sea, going round in circles. Fifteen–love to NATO – I think.

We were called one night to a Greek-registered vessel in the middle of Liverpool Bay. In those pre-GPS days, finding and identifying the right ship in the dark amongst all the sea traffic was not easy. When we were winched down and I was led down to the depths of the ship, there was a Pakistani seaman who had a collapsed lung. I decided we would take him to hospital in Liverpool. We had standing arrangements for this and a landing site at Walton Hospital at which we would be met by an ambulance. As we approached Liverpool, the Port Medical Officer came up on the radio, asking to speak to me and seeking more information about the patient. What was the problem? Why was his lung collapsed? Did he have tuberculosis? I didn't know why the lung had collapsed, but as far as I was concerned, tuberculosis would feature fairly high up my list of likely diagnoses, and should be considered a real possibility until proved otherwise.

The port MO ordered that the patient should not go the Walton Hospital, but rather to Fazackerly hospital, where he could be kept in isolation.

At the landing site we were met not just by the ambulance, but by two police cars, who led us on a fast blue-light dash across Liverpool to Fazackerly hospital. One car would dash ahead and stop all the traffic at the next junction. As we roared through, the second car would roar away and do the same. This continued for about twenty minutes. It wasn't strictly necessary on clinical grounds, but as they were having such fun it would have been a shame to stop them. When we got there we screeched to a stop, ran up to the door of the block to which we had been directed and which had the isolation ward on the first floor; and found it locked. We hammered on the door. After a bit an upstairs window opened, a head appeared and a female voice said "Ya what?" – or words to that effect. "It's us!" we shouted. "Helicopter in Rescue Drama." The head withdrew, the window was closed and it all went quiet.

The block looked like a typical Victorian hospital block, and I suspected, on the basis of assorted nefarious activities as a medical student, that at the far end there would be a small spiral staircase giving access to the far end of the ward, and that it would not be locked. That was indeed the case. I went up to the first floor and began to walk along the ward. I was still wearing my immersion flying suit and was aware that I must look a bit odd in the context. As I walked up the ward, a nurse approached, carrying a bedpan.

"'Who are you?"

"I'm Doctor McCoubrey, and…"

"Oh, that's all right then."

With which she turned off to the "sluice" to empty the bedpan.

But I did find someone to open the door and we were at last able to deliver our patient. Sadly we didn't have a blue-light ride back to the helicopter.

During the late 1970s, a number of AOCs had developed a habit that, when they were carrying out their Annual Formal

Inspection, they would instigate a simulated incident to test the station's response. In July 1978 it was Valley's turn. Shortly after he arrived, Air Vice Marshal Peter Bairsto announced that an aircraft had crashed on the station playing fields, taking out the railway bridge connecting the station to the medical centre as it did so. By pure chance I was making my way to the station at the time, with my airfield radio switched on. Hearing what was happening, and noticing that a bus had drawn up on the playing fields out of which were stepping a number of people made up as casualties, I diverted there. I started dealing with the casualties, having warned the medical centre what was happening and asking for help. As the bridge was for exercise purposes unusable, we would have to take casualties up to the bridge, carry them across the railway line, then reload them on the other side to take them to the medical centre. So I called the SAR flight, who agreed to provide a helicopter to ferry the casualties. All went well. When the helicopter returned to collect the last couple of casualties, it did so faster, lower, and more aggressively than seemed strictly necessary; especially with an Air Vice Marshal watching.

All soon became clear. The winchman came running from the helicopter towards me shouting, "Come on, Doc, we've got a call out and we need you." I thoroughly enjoyed turning to salute Peter Bairsto and saying, "Sorry, sir, I can't play your silly games any longer – I've got real work to do." Actually, I probably used different words, but the message was clear enough.

On one magical occasion I was on call for SAR while at a black tie party in the mess. We got a call to pick up an injured seaman from a fishing vessel near Valley. I had my kit in the boot of the car so I took off my dinner jacket, put on my immersion suit and was picked up by helicopter from the mess lawn. We collected and treated the casualty and took him to hospital. I was then dropped back on the mess lawn where I took off my immersion suit, put my DJ back on, smoothed my hair and rejoined the party. Sean Connery couldn't have done it better!

It wasn't always light-hearted. One Saturday morning we went to Tryfan in Snowdonia to pick up a man who had fallen about six feet off a rock. He hadn't fallen far, but had fractured his spine and was paralysed from the chest down. We were rather subdued on the way home.

As well as flying training, the students trained in combat survival and rescue, and I was involved in a number of exercises as part of this. "Exercise Shoulder Tapper" involved a student and his flying instructor being stopped immediately after landing, put in a helicopter and flown into darkest Snowdonia where they would have to survive overnight with only the equipment with which in theory they would have ejected. The safety precautions included the station combat survival and rescue officer and me being pre-positioned somewhere near where they were to be dropped. We too would spend the night there; but we had lots of kit in our Land Rover to ensure we were as comfortable as possible under the circumstances.

In a "standard" exercise, we would be in position and hiding behind a rock watching where the two participants were to be landed. They would be disembarked and, once the helicopter had gone, begin to shout obscenities at the surrounding countryside where they knew we would be hiding. We would go in and check them at dusk, refuse to help in any way, then leave them to it.

On one occasion our Land Rover got bogged down about half a mile short of our destination (our fault – don't blame those marvellous vehicles). We carried our stuff to our planned campsite and waited for the participants to arrive. They didn't, and at about half an hour before sunset an Army Air Corps helicopter flew in, told us the exercise had been cancelled and said we were free to return to Valley. We told them about the Land Rover and asked for a lift home. They refused, saying they had only just enough time to get back to Hampshire before the airfield at Middle Wallop closed. But they would let RAF Valley know what had happened. We were not best pleased – unlike most at Valley, who when they found out about it, thought it was one of the better examples of the revenge of fate.

It was a wild but reasonably comfortable night, given that we had all the latest survival kit. In the morning we were awakened by a strange whistling noise. Looking out of our tent, we saw a line of local shepherds, clad in what we would have described as totally unsuitable clothing, walking up the mountain rounding up their sheep. It was a timely reminder that the locals have learned over the years to cope with their conditions without having the benefits of modern science and expensive equipment.

We ran an escape and evasion exercise, during which the students would come across another crew who had ejected but had been injured. They had to demonstrate their first aid skills. I would look around for a couple of people to be the "ejectees", who would be made up as casualties and then treated many times as the various groups of students made their way through the exercise. On one occasion one of the station's WRAF officers volunteered to be a casualty. I explained to her that she would be dressed in flying kit, laid down on the ground and subjected to all sorts of invasions of her privacy by the students examining her. She convinced me that I had her informed consent. When the students approached the casualty, who was wearing a flying suit, helmet and oxygen mask, so being completely unrecognisable, they would invariably (and correctly) unzip the flying suit and thrust a hand in to check for injuries and a heartbeat. The looks on their faces at that point were an absolute picture. They clearly couldn't believe what was happening when I told them that they should carry on as normal. Interestingly, the young lady concerned seemed entirely content with what was going on.

Sometime in 1978 HRH The Prince of Wales visited Bardsey Island, off the Lleyn peninsula south-west of Anglesey. He was to arrive by a helicopter of The Queen's Flight and I was detailed to provide medical cover for his landing and take-off. The SAR flight delivered us (the dignitaries to receive HRH, assorted firemen and mechanics, and me) to await his arrival. I had been told that the basic rules for medical cover for Royal events were:

If the Royal personage realises that you are there hovering to pick up the pieces when it all goes wrong, you're dragged away to the Tower of London.

If the Royal personage trips, falls, faints or anything like that and you fail to catch them before they hit the ground, you're dragged away to the Tower of London.

So off I went to Bardsey in my flying suit and with my resuscitation kit and all the rest in a nondescript RAF blue holdall. The Royal helicopter arrived, while the SAR helicopter followed at a discreet distance. The Prince got out, was greeted by the Lord Lieutenant, and headed off with the official party towards the lighthouse. On the way he spotted the group of servicemen and turned towards us. He spoke to a few of them while I kept a low profile at the back. Then he looked me straight in the eye.

"You're the doctor, aren't you?"

"Er, yes, sir."

"And have you got the blood and stuff in that bag?"

"Er... yes, sir."

"Oh, good."

And he walked on; and I wasn't dragged away.

The visit went well, and after the Prince's departure one of the local fisherman appeared with a box of freshly caught crabs which he sold at a very good price to everyone still there. All in all, very different from a normal morning surgery.

I managed to get in quite a lot of flying in fixed wing aircraft as well. The flying instructors, as part of their continuation training, were required to carry out away landings and night stops at other airfields in the UK and overseas. The back seats were available for those keen enough to join them. I had a trip back to Bruggen, where my second SMO there, Wing Commander Ian Hourston, gave me a splendid weekend of reminiscing. We took three Gnats up to Leuchars on the Friday before a Scotland–Wales rugby international.

I had arranged with the SAR flight at Leuchars, one of whose pilots was about to come to Valley as the flight commander, to fly us down to Edinburgh the next morning and drop us in the grounds of Fettes, my old school. After we were dropped off, the other five headed off into central Edinburgh and a pub. I stayed a while to meet Dick Cole-Hamilton, my old housemaster. As we walked through the grounds, we chatted about how things had changed since I had been there. My all-boys school had just started taking girls; I wasn't quite sure whether I approved. Then a blonde vision walked past, wearing a well-filled cream silk blouse and sprayed-on black cords. "That's one of the girls," said Dick. I was converted.

When I joined the others, I found that we had had a stroke of luck. Our New Zealand exchange officer, Flight Lieutenant Frank Sharp, was one of the group. As the junior officer, he had been given the job of fighting his way through the scrum that forms in every Edinburgh pub on an international day and trying to get the drinks in. He had quickly discovered a barmaid who was not only also a Kiwi, but came from his home town. After that, drinks came quickly and cost £1 each.

Frank continued to be useful. On the way home, Leuchars SAR had agreed to pick us up from Turnhouse, but only if the weather was good enough. When we got there it was very foggy – we couldn't see the top of the control tower. We phoned Leuchars.

"How's the weather?" they asked.

"Er, not brilliant, but it seems to be clearing a bit." Winston Churchill would have called this a terminological inexactitude.

Five minutes or so later they called back. "We've tried to get off, but we're completely clagged in here. Sorry, you'll have to make your own way back."

We were perilously close to missing the last train from Edinburgh to Leuchars. Once we were on the bus from Turnhouse back to Edinburgh, Frank was dispatched to chat to the driver, to persuade him to get a move on. His colonial charm obviously worked. We drove past a number of bus stops leaving waiting passengers seething, and got to Haymarket station just in time. The train was full of very happy spectators from the match, so Frank organised some community singing in the carriage. As we crossed the Forth Bridge, he dozed off. When we got to Leuchars, he was still asleep. There was a suggestion that we should leave him undisturbed and let him wake up in Aberdeen; but because of his sterling efforts earlier we took pity on him and woke him up.

We had bought some MacSween's haggis in Edinburgh. For the flight back to Valley the next day they were stowed in the unpressurised luggage locker with our kit. Halfway home I had a terrible thought. I said to the pilot: "John, what happens if you decompress a haggis?" We had visions of opening the locker to find that the haggis had exploded, covering luggage and aircraft in a soggy mass of entrails. Fortunately they suffered no harm and were intact – and tasty as ever.

In the medical centre at Valley we would regularly receive casualties from the sea or Snowdonia who were suffering from exposure. To help treat them we had a specially raised bath, so that we could more easily work on the patient while they rewarmed. When we were warned of the arrival of an exposure casualty, the duty medical assistant would fill the bath with water at 42°C, the recommended temperature for rewarming. The casualty would be put in the bath as soon as they arrived, and resuscitation would begin. The duty medic would usually find himself tasked with cutting off the casualty's clothes. When one awakes from such an ordeal, one is rather confused. More than once I had to settle a significantly agitated lady, who awoke from a coma to find herself in a bath, surrounded by strangers, and with some man she'd never met cutting her clothes off.

Communications in those days were more basic. People who needed a "duty phone" had an extension on the station private branch exchange. This sometimes caused minor hiccups. Biddy Thornton, the station commander's wife, answered the phone in her married quarter one day to a wrong number.

"Is that the armoury?" said her interlocutor.

"No, it's the station commander's residence."

"Oh God."

"No, it's his wife."

Towards the end of our time at Valley, Flight Lieutenant David Cyster, one of the flying instructors, flew in his Tiger Moth from Britain to Australia, retracing the steps of Bert Hinckler, an Australian who had made the first solo flight from England to Australia in 1928. I prepared his emergency medical kit. He wanted it to "weigh nothing, occupy no space and cure everything". I was almost able to meet his specification. Our children were shown round his aircraft, and were greatly taken with his "pee tube", through which he relieved himself into the atmosphere while in flight. The station commander broadcast daily on the tannoy to keep us up to date with David's progress. Thailand and its holiday resorts weren't so well known in the 1970s, and his attempt to say the name "Phuket" in an acceptable manner produced a lot of laughs.

Valley was a very happy station, and a great place for young children. There was a long sandy beach by the side of the airfield, and Snowdonia was just up the road. However, sometimes the weather left a little to be desired. We regularly had heavy horizontal rain. Walking in a snow-covered Snowdonia one day Robin, who was wearing a snow suit with a shiny outer layer, fell over and was blown away, sliding like a toboggan over the snow. We caught up with him eventually. In our Station Standing Orders was an instruction always to park service vehicles pointing into wind; on a number of occasions cars parked otherwise had had their doors ripped off by a particularly fierce gust. So as well as the excitement and novelty of it all, the prospect of better weather appealed when I was told I was to be posted to Hong Kong.

4

Fragrant Harbour

The first thing to hit me about Hong Kong was the smell. As soon as the door of the RAF VC10 was opened at Kai Tak airport, a gust of warm humid air overlaid with the never-to-be-forgotten scent of whatever was rotting in the *nullah* beside the airfield rolled in and filled my nostrils.

We had flown out over twenty-four hours on an air trooping flight from Brize Norton in Oxfordshire, with a two-hour refuelling stop in Colombo. It was very basic and austere; there were no films and there was no alcohol. On the other hand, we were well cared for by the RAF cabin crew, who gave a real feeling of "looking after their own" and made it as comfortable as they could for us. And of course we were facing the rear of the aircraft, to give us a better chance of survival if there was a crash. For obvious reasons commercial airlines won't do this, but to an aviation medicine man it made perfect sense.

Previously, we had explained the whole expedition to the children. They sort of understood, although at the end of the explanation Robin, then aged three, asked if it involved leaving Anglesey.

At the time of the flight, Clare's "security blanket" was a pair of blue velvet trousers which had previously clothed a soft toy called

Jemima. Not long after take-off, "Jemima's trousers" fell between our seats and on to the floor. I couldn't find them. I looked to the row behind, where sat a (very) young Gurkha officer.

Me: "I don't suppose you can see Jemima's trousers on the floor, can you?"

VYGO: (Looks as horrified as only an unmarried twenty-two-year-old man can under the circumstances.)

Me: "It's just that, if we can't find them, we are likely to have a very unhappy five-year-old all the way to Hong Kong."

VYGO: (Rapidly finds trousers.) "Ah yes, here they are." Peace reigns; but VYGO continues to look horrified.

As we disembarked, a group of local baggage handlers was unloading our bags from the hold of the aircraft, chatting among themselves as they did so. Clare watched them for a few moments then announced, "They are talking Welsh." We decided to explain the difference later.

I was taking over from Warwick Pike, the hero of our arrival at Valley, and he met us at the airport and saw us to the hotel where we would spend our first few days. The RAF in Hong Kong had just undergone significant change, having been based at Kai Tak since first arriving in Hong Kong in the 1930s. A month or so earlier it had been moved out by the Hong Kong Government, who wanted all of its downtown space in Kowloon, to a new base at Sek Kong, up in the northern part of the New Territories. They had paid for the move, and also for the provision of new facilities at Sek Kong. We had a new headquarters building, hangars and workshops, and accommodation in a number of new low-rise blocks in the hills above the airfield. RAF Sek Kong was co-located with the Army's Gurkha Field Force, where I shared a medical centre and many medical duties with my Army opposite number. The two organisations were very different in ethos and operating procedures; we all had to do our bit to keep things working amicably.

There was a very small RAF presence in Hong Kong. The main operational unit was 28 (AC) Squadron, flying Wessex Helicopters.

AC stood for Army Cooperation – they provided helicopter support for army operations. More than once I heard "army cooperation" described as an oxymoron. As well as the usual station medical officer duties, my junior medical officer and I were on call six months of the year for Hong Kong wide helicopter search and rescue and casualty evacuation (casevac) – a role we shared with the Royal Hong Kong Auxiliary Air Force (RHKAAF).

The main justification for someone of my training and experience being in the job was as the Aeromedical Evacuation Co-ordinating Officer for the Far East. I was responsible for organising the aeromedical evacuation home of ill or injured British servicemen from an area roughly defined as east of Suez and west of San Francisco. My job was, as the job title indicated, to co-ordinate it all. Most of the work was done by my staff – a Flight Nursing Officer and a number of Flight Nursing Attendants, all specially trained for the task. It sounded glamorous, but mostly was just hard work. Squadron Leader Maggie Brown, my Flight Nursing Officer, once went to pick up an injured serviceman from Fiji, routing via New Zealand. It looks wonderful on paper, but she left Hong Kong at 1600 on a Monday, didn't get off the aircraft in New Zealand, had thirty minutes in Fiji going to and from the hospital to pick up the casualty, and arrived back in Hong Kong at 1000 on the Wednesday scarcely able to stand.

We arrived in Hong Kong towards the end of November, and were immediately swept up into what we at first assumed was the beginning of the Christmas party season. Fairly soon it became apparent that actually this was the norm for Hong Kong in those days. But I very soon hit a more sombre aspect of it all.

The 22nd of December 1978 was a Friday; at lunchtime the Officers' Mess at RAF Sek Kong were entertaining the Sergeants' Mess to drinks – a traditional way to begin the Christmas break. As I entered the bar with John Wood, my medical centre sergeant, Squadron Leader Malcolm Pledger, who commanded 28 Squadron, approached us. Had I heard about the boat? The boat in question was the *Huey Fong*, a tatty old merchant ship with about 3000 Vietnamese refugees on board. She was headed for Hong Kong, and the squadron had been told to stand by and await developments. This was the first refugee ship of a significant size to come to Hong Kong and we were not sure what would happen, or what conditions might be like on board. We suspected that there might be quite a few sick people and that we would be asked to carry out helicopter casualty evacuation.

The *Huey Fong* arrived just outside Hong Kong waters on Christmas Eve. There she anchored, since the government had refused her permission to enter the territory. A message from the ship indicated that those on board were short of food and water. 28 Squadron was given the job of transferring the supplies to the boat; at that stage the government did not want any ships going alongside.

I went down to the squadron after church (it was a Sunday), to see what was going on. I asked if I could ride in one of the helicopters so as to have a good look at the *Huey Fong*, since I might well get involved with casualties and I wanted to assess the situation I would have to work with. The squadron was short of crews, as apart from the duty crew a fair number of people were away on leave or scattered about Hong Kong. They were being recalled, but numbers were still short. I didn't realise how short until we were halfway out to the *Huey Fong* when I was asked, "I say, Doc, I don't suppose you'd mind going on to the boat and arranging the unloading and distribution of stores, would you? We're a bit short of crewmen, you see."

Under the circumstances there wasn't much I could do but agree. So I spent my Christmas Eve aboard the *Huey Fong*, organising the refugees into parties to help me grab and unload the underslung loads of food and other essentials which were being ferried out by helicopter. We had only a small area on the roof of the aft cabins on which to work; and one load more than covered it. I had to organise human chains to pass the food for storage in other parts of the boat.

The refugees were crammed together like sardines – it was literally standing room only. They seemed totally apathetic and looked at me with expressionless faces. It reminded me of some of the WWII newsreels which show Jews being herded off to the gas chambers.

In the middle of the afternoon I got a garbled message that a woman was giving birth somewhere on board. There was a contingent of Royal Hong Kong Police on board (to prevent any foolish attempts at sailing into Hong Kong waters and also, as far as I was concerned, to ensure my safety). With their aid we passed a message to send a casevac helicopter to take her (or if it was too late, them) off. Because of the constant flow of supplies coming on board I couldn't leave my platform. I asked them to bring the woman to me. It was just as well, I thought, that they had a doctor for a loadmaster.

When the woman was brought to me, she had already been safely delivered of a baby girl. Although both looked well, the *Huey Fong* was no place for them, so when an Alouette helicopter of the RHKAAF arrived, I was very relieved. The mother was winched up in a Neil-Robertson stretcher. After we had wondered for a bit how to take up the baby, the solution, in the shape of a wicker basket, was produced by one of the refugees.

Towards evening I was relieved on the platform by one of the squadron crewmen and returned home for a belated lunch. When I told the children about the baby, it being Christmas Eve, and Clare being full of the Nativity story, she was rather disappointed that there had been neither angels nor shepherds. Although the squadron continued to resupply over the Christmas period, I was not myself involved again until New Year's night. At about 11pm I was called to casevac from the boat a fifty-five-year-old man with internal bleeding. It wasn't the best of nights. The wind was fairly strong and the sea concomitantly rough. It was of course dark, and the Police were no longer on board. The Hong Kong government was anxious lest the refugees should try to take a hostage, and we were told not to detach ourselves from the helicopter while carrying out the casevac. This was virtually impossible, so the crewman who was going down with me and I evolved an anti-hostage plan (!) One of us would always keep an eye on the refugees, and we would keep them clear of our direct route to the side of the boat. At any sign of trouble we would leap off the boat into the sea. It may have been rough and dark, but we were wearing the appropriate survival equipment and there was a helicopter with a winch nearby.

In the event there was no trouble of that sort. The patient they produced didn't seem to have any of the symptoms I had expected, but as he was obviously suffering from shock, we loaded him on to the stretcher and he was winched up. As this was going on, the refugees produced another two patients, one a young child, whom they also wanted us to take. This was getting slightly ridiculous, but as both looked very ill I agreed to take them.

The crewman came back down to pick me up with the news that none of these was the patient we had originally come for. It appeared that he had died. The refugees wanted us to wait while they brought us the body to be taken away. At this point we had to say no. The situation was hazardous enough to both the helicopter and ourselves as it was, without waiting with our three patients until we were brought someone for whom we could do nothing. Anxiously, in case they should turn nasty, we refused. We were winched back to the helicopter and took the patients to hospital. A helicopter returned early next morning to remove the corpse.

This sort of situation was obviously unsatisfactory, and it came as no surprise when the Master of the *Huey Fong* asked next day, via the ship-to-shore radio, to meet some people to discuss medical problems. I was detailed to go and next afternoon found myself being winched on board HMS Monkton, where her captain, Lieutenant Paul Wainwright RN, and I were to meet the Master and three representatives of the refugees. My brief was simple. I could promise nothing but to pass messages and make recommendations to the Hong Kong government.

We were joined shortly after I arrived by the Master and three refugees who claimed to be a former Medical Officer, Pharmacist and Nurse in the South Vietnamese army. Their demands for medical supplies and description of the hygienic conditions on board were exactly as I had expected. There was a lot of non-specific diarrhoea, people had infected cuts and sores, and there was a lot of respiratory tract infection. They asked for drugs to treat this and for a safe water supply, since their cookers were in almost constant use boiling what water they had. All this was obviously reasonable, and I agreed to recommend to government that these should be supplied. That part of the discussion took about ten minutes.

For the next hour and three quarters they went on to make various political demands and arguments. Neither Paul Wainwright nor I was authorised to do anything about that, so we continued to push the government line that the *Huey Fong* should sail on to Taiwan, its first scheduled port of call. We didn't get very far along this road before they put forward another suggestion: that they be allowed into Hong Kong purely as a holding point before being resettled elsewhere. This was a new development and Paul Wainwright went off to radio this to the shore. He and I had agreed that neither of us would say anything remotely connected with the business of the day while the other was absent. The eyes of the world were on Hong Kong and the *Huey Fong* and neither he nor I wanted to be in the middle of some political row which we might be accused of causing.

I asked the refugees about their past and the voyage. They were obviously overwrought, but equally obviously sincere refugees fleeing from a real threat. The Medical Officer, who was my age, had a daughter the same age as mine. She and his wife were on board the *Huey Fong*. He was an ex-Captain. Apart from the fact that his country had been conquered and so he had missed out on promotion, our lives really had quite a lot in common. That little five-minute chat, more than anything, brought home to me the horror of the whole Vietnamese refugee crisis.

When Paul reappeared with the government's rejection of the proposals, the refugees broke down and wept. We weren't sure how much was real and how much for effect. Shortly after that the Nurse hinted that if they weren't allowed to land in Hong Kong, they would all throw themselves in the sea and drown. This was a threat we had heard from them several times in the previous few days. Having spent two hours getting to know them, I didn't believe that they would, and said so in a joking manner. To my surprise the Nurse grinned rather shamefacedly and agreed that of course they wouldn't. So at least one gain had been made from the meeting – that particular threat had been shown to be hollow.

The meeting adjourned, the refugees were taken back to their ship and I was flown ashore. By this time I was seen as something of an expert on the *Huey Fong* and was sent for to brief a number of people on the subject. Most surprisingly, I was even asked to talk to the then Defence Secretary, Fred Mulley – (in)famous for having fallen asleep while sitting beside the Queen at a Royal review of the RAF – while he passed through Hong Kong.

In the end, of course, the refugees were allowed ashore, and were followed by about 60,000 others. The *Huey Fong* was seized, and the Hong Kong government spent a long time searching it for the gold which had been paid for the voyage and which everyone knew the Master must have somewhere on board. Nothing was found until the ship was being broken up. The gold had been beaten into thin sheet, wrapped round the propeller shaft and covered with grease. Fortunately it was discovered just before being melted down with the rest of the metal.

The Vietnamese "boat people" were the first of what seems to be an ever-increasing number of seaborne refugees. We are inured to them now, and their numbers dwarf those we saw in 1979. But it was interesting to be in at the beginning of it all.

After the drama of the *Huey Fong* life at Sek Kong settled back to normal. It was a very pleasant existence, although for much of the summer the heat and humidity was overbearing. I didn't have many

RAF patients or families to look after, so in addition I cared for the locally engaged Chinese workers and their families whose contracts included receiving medical care. I would hold clinics with Annie Wat, a Hong Kong Chinese nurse who acted as translator. As time passed I picked up enough Cantonese to ask the basic questions; and if I got standard answers I was all right. But I never got beyond that and would regularly have to turn to Annie for help.

I ran an antenatal clinic for the Chinese families. It was a somewhat irregular affair, for many of the women lived subsistence farmers' lives in the farms and fishing villages in the surrounding area, and they tended to turn up when they felt like it rather than at what I would have considered an appropriate stage in their pregnancy. As a result, the numbers attending varied dramatically. On one never-to-be-forgotten day I returned from lunch to find the whole medical centre absolutely teeming with pregnant Chinese women, with Annie trying to establish some sort of order. Somewhat taken aback, and without thinking, I said, "Annie, what on earth have they all been doing?" Annie immediately translated this into Cantonese for the benefit of the patients, who roared with laughter at the thought of the Gweilo Yee-san not even knowing how they got pregnant. There was much giggling throughout the rest of the clinic.

Every second month we were on call for casevac. On a typical call-out I would go over to the squadron with my kit – although in theory you knew what you were going for, it was often not quite as advertised – and off we would go to a remote area or outlying island to pick up a casualty or seriously ill patient to transfer them to hospital. Flying out I would sit and look out the door at the wonderful scenery. Once we had delivered the patient to hospital, I would usually climb up into the co-pilot's seat and fly the helicopter home. From time to time I would reflect that not only was I being paid to do this, but I was receiving an extra allowance to cope with the extra costs of Hong Kong. I felt very grateful for it all.

Some casevacs were more memorable than others. We were called to the Gurkhas' training depot, to pick up a young recruit who appeared to be suffering from heatstroke. I got an intravenous line running before we put him in the helicopter, and off we went. Halfway to hospital the rehydration had its effect and the patient began to recover consciousness. It is normal to be a little confused when you wake up under these circumstances. When this young Gurkha trainee, who had only been out of Nepal for about three weeks, awoke in the noisy, vibrating back of the helicopter, with a strange green creature with a green shiny ball instead of a face (I had my flying suit and helmet on, with the tinted visor down) kneeling over him, he reacted as only a member of a fierce warrior race would. He tried to kill me. We weren't quite ready for this. The cabin door was open and we were at risk of being thrown out; and he was very fit and aggressive. In the end I was forced to use the highly sophisticated medical technique of kneeling on his throat to subdue him. It worked. We got him safely to hospital and he made a full recovery.

We shared casevac on alternate months with the RHKAAF, but there was a bit of give and take. During one of their duty months, the RHKAAF got a call to go to a very large tanker in the South China Sea, out of range but pointing directly at Hong Kong. The request was to pick up a seaman with serious back injuries as soon as they could get within range. The RHKAAF had just received two new Dauphin helicopters and were very keen to show off to the government what a wise purchase that had been. To that end they were planning to send one of their fixed wing aircraft, laden with pressmen and cameras, to film the recovery of the casualty. The RHKAAF had their own medical officer, who was an anaesthetist in one of the private hospitals. He was a thoroughly competent clinician, but not as experienced in casevac work as I was. He asked if I would stand in for him.

So off we went. We found the *Cast Petrel* easily enough. Having prepared myself for all the cameras in the following aircraft, I was winched down on to the ship. A man was standing there waiting to meet me. This didn't always happen, so I was rather pleased, especially when he spoke English. I explained that I was a doctor, and had come to pick up the casualty with serious back injuries. He announced that he was that casualty. Ah. I indicated the circling aircraft with the cameras and asked if he would mind awfully lying down so that I could put him in a stretcher and have him winched up to the helicopter. He was entirely happy with this. So it all came to pass, and that night's RTHK news led with film of the dramatic rescue from a ship in the South China Sea using the very wonderful new helicopters provided by the munificent Hong Kong government. Remember this incident every time you watch the television news.

Although my staff did most of the aeromedical evacuation work, I would take the odd trip myself. They tended to be short ones – I couldn't be away for too long – and interesting (or I wouldn't have gone). During my time in Hong Kong the RAF stopped providing airlift to and from Nepal for the Gurkhas, and Nepal Airlines were given a contract to provide the service. There was the odd "reverse aeromed" where we would take a sick Gurkha home at the end of his engagement to continue treatment in Nepal. We had a plan to rig stretchers in the cabin and provide all the care he might need, but the first time we actually did it I decided to go myself. It also gave me a chance to see something of Nepal and get a feeling for what medical care was actually available in Kathmandu and elsewhere. Flying east from Kathmandu to visit the British Military Hospital in Dharan, I was somewhat embarrassed when the cabin staff insisted I should have the best seat in the aircraft to see Mount Everest as we flew past. But it was worth it.

There was a battalion of Gurkhas in Brunei. We got a call from the young RAMC captain who was their medical officer asking for the very urgent evacuation of a Gurkha with schizophrenia. There were no British service aircraft available so, because of the urgency, I got permission to travel by civil airline. The first flight out was with Cathay Pacific Airlines, many of whose pilots I knew through having carried out their annual medicals. The first flight back after that, the next day, was with Royal Brunei Airlines. I took with me my corporal flight nursing attendant, chosen because he was the largest and strongest member of my staff.

We got there and assessed the patient, who wasn't actually schizophrenic, but was certainly disturbed. Having made arrangements to collect him and my corporal the next day, I was taken off to the Shell Oil social club, which was used by the British Army staff in Brunei. Halfway across its swimming pool I came across a man going the other way. We looked at each other and after a couple of seconds I realised he was Gordon Duff, who had been in my year at medical school, and who was now working for Shell. The rest of the day was spent happily reminiscing and celebrating the serendipity.

Next morning we set out for the airport. You must remember that this was 1979 and things, especially flying, were very different from the way they are now. If you take a sick person on a commercial airline you are supposed to talk to the airline and liaise with their authorities so that everyone is clear as to what is happening and that no one is put at risk. That's the theory. I had been advised from a couple of sources that at that time Royal Brunei's attitude to mental health problems was not perhaps as modern as it might be, so I made the executive decision not to tell them anything, but just to travel back in a row of three seats, with Mr McCoubrey on the inside, Mr Gurung (the Gurkha) in the middle and Mr Smith (my corporal) on the outside. I carried with me a syringe loaded with a knockout mixture. If the patient got too wobbly, I would give the word to my corporal, who would hold him down while I stuck the needle in his thigh and injected him. Then we would play it by ear. You could do things like that then.

It started fairly well, although the patient was given a hard time by the Brunei immigration staff; there was a long history of racial dislike between Malays and Gurkhas. But we got on board and all was well until they served us lunch. The corporal and I selected our choice of main course, but as the patient couldn't read we asked the cabin staff just to serve him whatever, which was a mistake on my part. Shortly after starting to eat, the patient announced, "This is beef," (which was of course taboo to him).

Me: "Er, no, no. It's, er, Astrakhan Lamb."

Corporal (demonstrating why he's a corporal rather than a squadron leader): "No sir, it's beef. It says so here on the menu." (Indicates.)

Patient: (Splutters and begins to wobble.)

Me: "No, corporal, you are wrong. It is definitely Astrakhan Lamb. As an officer I am certain of this."

Patient: (Looks slightly relieved. He has been trained and trained and trained to believe that an officer is *always* right.)

Corporal (realising): "Gosh, you're right, sir. How silly of me. Of course it's Astrakhan Lamb."

Everyone settles down and the patient finishes his lunch.

It is a mark of how things were in those days that, had the patient not settled and I had had to subdue him, I did not foresee any problems on arrival at Hong Kong. I would merely have announced myself as the Senior RAF Medical Officer accompanying a sick soldier and all would have been cleared to let us through. This "colonial" (and not always entirely admirable) attitude was omnipresent. A colleague who commanded the RAF movements unit at Kai Tak was driving home early one morning, in uniform, having seen off a couple of transport aircraft. He rounded a corner and stopped at traffic lights. He realised as he did so that in the next lane there was a bent motorcycle with a bleeding Chinese man lying beside it. He got out to see what needed to be done. As he did so, a police Land Rover also came round the corner, saw the scene, and stopped. My colleague was slightly anxious as to what might happen next. There was no need. The Royal Hong Kong Police officer looked at the injured motorcyclist, then at my colleague in uniform, and said, "Is this man giving you any trouble sir?" My colleague, who had a sound conscience, very nearly hit him for his blatant prejudice.

There were some advantages. I had been to an Old Fettesian Dinner in the Hong Kong Club, and was driving home to the New Territories in the early morning with more alcohol in my blood than was sensible; but I knew the police wouldn't bother me. I was listening to the radio and heard of the unmasking of Anthony Blunt as a traitor. Driving home under the influence after an old boys' dinner and learning of treachery within the Establishment seemed to be an encapsulation of much that was wrong with society then. But it was an interesting experience.

Hong Kong was (and is) an exotic place. We had all sorts of visitors, especially during the late autumn when the climate was at its most bearable and it was a good time for Christmas shopping. There were regular top table lunches in the mess to welcome them. During my spell as President of the Mess Committee, and with the help of the mess sergeant, I learned a lot about chilled soups, which I still enjoy today.

The Prince of Wales came to visit the Second Goorkhas (as they spelled themselves). He travelled about Hong Kong by helicopter. I had to be at the landing ground as he took off, and at the next one as he landed, which required me to be dashing about in a second helicopter, overtaking him after take-off and being ready for his arrival. Setting it all up required a bit of reconnaissance. While driving about doing so I got rammed from behind by a large lorry, giving me a whiplash injury to my neck. It soon got better, but forty years later it has come back to bother me with a vengeance.

I worked daily with the Army; but of course the Royal Navy were in Hong Kong too. Their Medical Director General, Surgeon Vice-Admiral Sir John Rawlins, visited them at their base on Hong Kong harbour, and expressed an interest in seeing the New Territories. I was tasked with showing him round, and we gave him lunch in our flat at Sek Kong. Out Filipina house girl, Ella, was somewhat disappointed by him. Told to expect an admiral, she was rather looking forward to a wooden leg and a parrot.

In return John Rawlins invited us to join what he called a

"run ashore" – an evening out – just before he left. We started off "aboard HMS Tamar". This was in fact in the flat of Captain Bob Moland, the Captain-in-Charge, Hong Kong, in a tower block on the harbour-side. We then went aboard the Captain's Barge and went to eat at a floating restaurant. And they still called it a "run ashore". How the Navy does mangle the language.

We became friendly with the assistant American Air Attaché, Major Larry Mitchell, and his wife Sally. I had worked with Larry when Vice President Mondale had visited Hong Kong, and Malcolm Pledger and I spent a weekend with Larry aboard one of our helicopters, following "Fritz" Mondale about and ready to dash in and grab him if anything went wrong. It didn't, and we had a happy weekend playing with more communications equipment than I could have thought ever existed.

The Commander RAF Hong Kong for most of my time there was Group Captain Tom Bennett. He and his wife Anthoula had no children, which seemed a great shame, because in Hong Kong he was everyone's favourite grandfather. On Christmas Day Air House was an open house to all his officers and their families. In the hall was a vast bowl of sweets to which children were invited to help themselves as often as they liked, but only when they had finished the previous one. It is a mark of the man that none of them cheated, and all had their fill. Our children still talk about it.

Tom Bennett had recommended to me a book called *Sagittarius Rising*, by Cecil Lewis. It is a seminal description of life as a pilot in the First World War. Towards the end, Lewis describes his going to China after the war, to train Chinese pilots. He writes at some length about an American colleague called Pat Patterson. One evening at dinner at the Mitchells, I met an old American pilot called Pat Patterson, who talked of teaching the Chinese to fly shortly after the First World War. I immediately connected him with Cecil Lewis' story, and said so. His response was extraordinary. He vigorously, angrily even, denied all knowledge of what I was talking about, and said it was nothing to do with him. I changed the subject rapidly. Despite asking around afterwards I never found out why he was so agitated or whether he was in fact the same man. It remains one of life's continuing mysteries.

Vivien took her turn running the RAF Sek Kong wives' club. More in hope than expectation, she wrote to Radio Hong Kong to ask if they would broadcast one of their *Any Questions* programmes from Sek Kong. They agreed, and I was given the job of liaising between them and the station. They asked if they could have an RAF representative on the panel. Tom Bennett was the obvious choice, but when I asked him he not only refused but ordered me to fill the slot. Of course I had to be totally non-political. Most of the questions were fairly easy to deal with, but just before the end we were asked what we thought would happen to Hong Kong after 1997, when the British lease of the New Territories came to an end. My answer was that not only would it continue, but that its effect would probably spread northward up into what we then called Shum Chun. Today as I look at Shenzhen and all that is there I feel pleased I was right about the economic expansion, whatever the overall state of Hong Kong.

We saw in the 1980s on a boat in Hong Kong Harbour with my mother and mother-in-law, both of whom came to visit. We had a long weekend in Manila, with "space available" seats kindly provided by a friend who flew for Cathay Pacific, happily leaving the children with Ella. And we had a wonderful family holiday in Singapore and Malaysia, driving up through the Malaysian peninsula and having a week on the beach in Penang. But we knew it was lotus-eating. At the end of 1980 we had to return to UK.

5

Seeking Higher Things

Lincolnshire can be bleak at the best of times. In November, with the wind whistling straight from the Urals to blow across the Fens, it's seriously bleak. Coming there from the balmy late autumn of Hong Kong was a distinct shock to the system. The children felt it especially; Robin, who had left UK aged three, had no real concept of being cold.

However, despite the weather, I was rather pleased to be posted to Cranwell. It was a bigger job than I had anticipated at this stage in my career. I had more staff, more responsibilities, and of course more challenges. And I rather enjoyed all the ceremonial: magnificent dining-in nights in College Hall Officers' Mess, with a bugler in the minstrels' gallery playing the Post-horn Gallop on a rifle with a mouthpiece in the muzzle: passing-out parades where proud cadets marched off up the steps of College Hall into the Rotunda as newly commissioned officers, watched by proud families and other happy bits of pomp and circumstance.

As at Valley, I was taking over from John Baird. Also as at Valley we wouldn't both be there for a handover. By now, however, we knew each other and our various ways fairly well and he was able to leave a brief for me to pick up on arrival.

The RAF College had changed in the eight years since I had

last been there. It undertook all RAF Initial Officer Training (IOT), and there were various other departments for postgraduate officer training. There was still, of course, a flying training school, but it looked as though my opportunities for getting airborne would be limited.

Sociologically it had changed as well. There was no one left who had fought in WWII (although Air Vice-Marshal Desmond Hughes, who had been the Commandant during my first tour at Cranwell, lived locally and was still a member of the College shoot, where I would see him from time to time). Significantly, there was a marked increase in the number of female personnel. I was particularly aware of this as all my "airmen" below NCO rank were in fact airwomen, and two of my three junior medical officers were female.

I had been appointed a General Practice trainer before going to Hong Kong. However, training my one trainee in the relaxed atmosphere out there was very different from training three hard-worked juniors at Cranwell. Furthermore, in such a large and varied station my involvement in wider occupational medicine beyond "pure" aviation medicine was significantly greater. It was all quite hard work.

The warming up of the cold war during the late 1970s had resulted in the College carrying out various "survival to operate" exercises, which certainly wouldn't have been allowed to disturb the serenity of its existence during my previous tour. Fortunately I was able to avoid the worst of the hassle associated with playing war games in a training and spit and polish environment. My war role was as medical adviser to the Regional Commander who would run our bit of the country in the event of WWIII and a nuclear strike. When an exercise was called, the Regional Commander's staff, led by the Chief of Staff Group Captain Bobby Robson, whose day job was as the Director of IOT, disappeared into our appointed bunker "somewhere in eastern England", where we did little but check communications, chat and play cards.

The chat wasn't entirely mindless – we often chewed the fat

about problems at work. Bobby Robson was worried about the high incidence of injuries during IOT. Apart from the fact we didn't like breaking people, there was the problem of lost training time and, at worst, cadets having to repeat the course. Cadets weren't keen on this, and neither was the College, not least because of the additional costs it generated. My junior medical officers didn't like it either, and were not slow in advancing their opinion that the IOT course was too physically demanding, with cadets being injured unnecessarily.

To get a feel for what cadets actually experienced, I accompanied one course on their advanced leadership training camp which took place over a week at the Otterburn training area in Northumberland. On each exercise I accompanied a different Flight, so as to get as wide an overview as possible. I don't think they arranged it as such, but it seemed to me that whichever Flight I was with decided that, as part of their solution to whatever the problem was, they had to sprint up the nearest hill. It was very tiring. On one exercise I got sufficiently worn out that, while they regrouped and planned their next move, I lay down to rest on the heather. I was somewhat taken aback when they decided that I was having a heart attack, and were all for implementing the various emergency procedures. Fortunately, I was able to convince them that my only problem was that I was knackered.

It was all a bit anecdotal, however, so I carried out a survey to look at injuries occurring in three IOT courses – a total of 395 people – over a period of seven months in 1981. We were able to identify the activities most likely to cause injury, the types of injury that were most likely to result and the probable cause of those injuries. Although there were a number of factors, it soon became apparent that the chief culprit was the boots issued to the cadets on arrival. Directly Moulded Sole (DMS) boots were the standard issue to the British Armed Forces. They were sturdy and long-lasting. But they were not made of the finest, most supple leather, and they required some breaking in. The leather itself was tough and the spine at the back of the boot, deliberately rigid to give support, was rather unyielding when first worn.

Once the boots were broken in, there was much less trouble. Blisters and Achilles Tendonitis (inflammation at the back of the ankle) were much less common later on in the course, even when the activities became more strenuous. I proposed a simple solution, with which Bobby Robson agreed. Cadets should be issued with their boots some time before arrival at Cranwell, together with instructions on how to break them in.

We had reckoned without the objections from administrators and financiers. Where would the boots be sent? How could we ensure that the cadets would carry out the instructions? Had the instructions for breaking in the boots been cleared with the appropriate training agency? How could we be certain that this novel and contentious plan would work? Wicked people might keep the boots and not report for training, thus occasioning a loss to the public purse. And so on. We set to work to counter all the objections, but had other plans for the interim.

We reviewed and adjusted some of the activities which caused greater number of injuries. We improved the training of new IOT flight commanders. These young officers, from all branches of the RAF, had usually never been involved in supervising strenuous physical exercises such as they had to now. It was notable that formal physical education classes, carried out by a qualified physical education officer, produced very few injuries.

Part of the improved training was a lecture by me on the medical aspects of running a course such as IOT. I was the first to admit that this might not be the most exciting part of their day, so I did my best to liven it up a bit. My favourite gambit was to mention ladies' inside leg measurements. This usually woke up the boys although it tended to produce a look of anxiety on the faces of the girls. It is in fact highly relevant to drill. The standard RAF marching pace, as defined in Air Publication 818, the RAF Manual of Drill, is 30 inches (750mm) long. On average (and we had this data from our anthropometric measurements), female cadets were four and a half inches shorter than male cadets. This meant that in general their legs were that much shorter as well. As a result, when marching with a standard pace, they had to stretch out more, putting additional strain on their legs and feet. This wasn't just a theory – my survey had shown that women were 2.7 times more likely to suffer an injury than men. As well as keeping the new flight commanders awake, I think it put the necessary message across.

We immediately began training the cadets in breaking in their boots, and supplied them with Neatsfoot Oil to condition the leather. Although the system had grudgingly agreed to provide this, it took some time for formal approval and Bobby Robson bought the first batch out of his own pocket.

Injuries did indeed decrease and in time we won over the objectors. Shortly after I left Cranwell, a "Boots Weekend" was introduced. Cadets came to the College for a couple of days about a month before their course and were issued with their boots and instructions for breaking them in. Various other administrative actions were carried out at the same time, as a result of which the cadets could literally hit the ground running when they started the course proper. And overall it was very cost effective. Bobby Robson and I were very pleased.

The flying training school produced its usual run of aviation medicine problems for my attention, and we were lucky to have based at Cranwell a Medical Officer Pilot, Wing Commander Shaun Marshall, who undertook remedial flying with those who suffered intractable airsickness. I did my bit for flight safety. *Air Clues*, the RAF flight safety magazine, published a monthly column called "I learnt about flying from that" in which people recounted incidents from their flying career which didn't go exactly according to plan, but which they survived and from which lessons could be learnt. I wrote up a couple from my own experience and was very pleased when they were published.

One unusual bit of flying training provided me with a

particularly memorable three weeks. HRH Prince Edward was to learn to fly in the summer after he had left Gordonstoun (and was waiting for his A level results; even Princes have to suffer that). Arrangements had been made for a flying training course to be held at RAF Barkston Heath, a small airfield near Cranwell used as a relief landing ground when the airfield at Cranwell got very busy. I was attached to the course as the medical officer, to look after both clinical and aviation medicine aspects of care. It was a very relaxed and happy group. A number of University Air Squadron cadets had been nominated to join us to provide a mixture of student pilots, and the flying instructors, all specially selected, had just the right balance of support and control.

There were various arrangements to ensure the Prince's safety. Whenever he flew solo I was required to be in the air traffic control tower in case of need. There wasn't any such case, and I spent much of the time looking out over Lincolnshire and listening to the air traffic chat on the radio. Security had of course been enhanced for the Prince's visit, and people were particularly on edge because it was not long after Michael Fagan had broken into Buckingham Palace and entered the Queen's bedroom.

One afternoon I was using binoculars to watch some hares playing on the far side of the airfield. A movement in the hedge behind them caught my eye. When I looked more closely I could see a man carrying a gun. I thought I knew what was going on, but you can't take chances. I pointed him out to the Prince's personal protection officer, who was in the tower with me. He immediately radioed the nearby Lincolnshire Constabulary quick-reaction squad. A minute or so later we saw four armed police burst through the hedge and throw the gunman to the ground.

His weapon was a shotgun, and of course what he was doing was (in his own words) "a bit o' poachin' ". We were, after all, in Lincolnshire. There was much laughter in the tower and the poacher, who had a perfectly legally held shotgun, was let off with a warning.

At the end of the course we all went off to a nearby pub for a celebration meal. The personal protection officer had been to check it out, and to explain to the landlord what was happening. The landlord obviously took it very seriously. We were much amused to find that the waiters serving us all wore white gloves – probably the first and last time that had happened.

During my time at Cranwell the Argentinian invasion of the Falkland Islands took place. It provided an opportunity to see some action and I bothered my headquarters staff to see if they could find a role for me in the RAF's response. Of course they couldn't, and pointed out that the units deployed had their own medical officers, and also that I was already doing an important job. As I suppose I was. Despite this, I very much wanted to get involved. As it happened, quite soon I was, even if only indirectly.

Cranwell was my third tour as an SMO on a flying station and I felt that I needed to broaden my experience if my career was to progress as I hoped it would. While at Valley I had completed the Individual Staff Studies course, an eighteen-month distance-learning course to teach the rudiments of staff work. I now started asking through the relevant channels to be considered for selection for the Advanced Staff Course at the RAF Staff College. Competition for this was fierce, as there was only one place on the course each year for a member of the medical services. I was delighted, therefore, to be told that I had been selected for the Advanced Staff Course beginning in February 1983.

It wasn't quite as simple as that, however. The "postings plot", which moves officers about the RAF to fill vacancies left by resignations, retirements and return from overseas as well as moves for training and widening of experience, had my replacement at Cranwell, Group Captain Robin Davie, coming back from Cyprus to take up the SMO post in December 1982. I knew that I would be sent off somewhere to fill one of the manning gaps which appear from time to time. What I didn't expect was that the gap would be on Ascension Island.

6

Ascension

Ascension Island was discovered by the Portuguese explorer Alfonso de Albuquerque on Ascension Day 1501. It was dry and barren, and had little appeal for mariners, so he didn't claim it for the Portuguese crown. It is the tip of an inactive volcano rising from the mid-Atlantic ridge, and most of its thirty-four square miles are a lunar-type landscape consisting of clinker.

It was claimed for King George III on 22nd October 1815, when it was garrisoned by the British as a precaution after imprisoning Napoleon on St Helena, some 800 miles to the south-east. Charles Darwin visited it during his voyage in HMS Beagle, and it was a staging post for the Eastern Telegraph Company's cable from Britain to South Africa. NASA extended the WWII runway on Wideawake airfield as an emergency landing site for the Space Shuttle (which never used it), and there were a number of radio monitoring stations. But apart from that it was all very isolated and peaceful until 1982.

After the Argentine invasion in April 1982, Britain put together a task force to retake the Falkland Islands and South Georgia. Ascension Island, halfway between UK and the Falklands, was used as a staging post. Personnel and supplies could be flown to the island, to be picked up by ships passing through. Perhaps the best known actions from Ascension during the Falklands War were the "Black Buck" missions, in which Vulcan bombers from Ascension flew to and from the Falklands to bomb the airfield at Port Stanley. This involved a large number of air-to-air refuellings, not only of the bombers but of the refuelling aircraft themselves, and was a great feat of planning, flying skill and rapid technological advance driven by wartime necessity. At the time they were the longest-range bombing raids in history.

By the time I arrived on the 6th of December 1982 the war had been over for six months. Although we were still in theory on alert for a possible attempt by Argentina to continue the conflict, no one seriously thought this was remotely likely.

The vast influx of British troops and materiel meant that we had tented camps and stores all over the island. It felt and looked a bit like a frontier town and there were moves to get the whole military presence into a more orderly shape. Many things ran on a "needs must" basis. Perhaps the most immediately obvious example was in accounting for vehicle fuel. On a normal RAF station, fuel was scrupulously monitored, with costs and usage being noted for every vehicle and section. On Ascension, the airman who ran the filling station would, each Monday, write down the total amount of fuel he held and add to it any deliveries. Above that he would write the amount of fuel he had had the previous Monday. The first was subtracted from the second, and that was fuel usage accounted for. It looks slack, but the small size of the island, the very limited number of roads and the fact that there was in effect nowhere to go ensured that there was no possibility of misuse.

The US Air Force ran the airfield – although apart from a USAF Lieutenant Colonel as base commander, all the personnel were civilian contractors. NASA and Cable and Wireless, the other two large presences on the island, were part of a joint enterprise which provided support services, including medical care. The "civil power" – the Administrator – was an FCO man who reported to the Governor of St Helena. Professionals and technicians tended to be expatriates; support staff were mostly St Helenians – always known as "Saints" – employed on contract.

The USAF had two medical technicians, who coped with the vast majority of their minor and self-limiting illnesses. In Georgetown, the island capital, there was a small hospital manned by a GP, Robin Whitla, who could give anaesthetics, and a surgeon, Raj Sukhtankar. I had the use of the USAF "dispensary" – in effect a treatment room – for one hour a day, during which we could change dressings and do other things which required clinical cleanliness and needed to be out of the constant wind and dust of the island; and I could admit patients to the hospital if they needed to be bedded down.

The medical section was based in a caravan by the airfield and we had a chilled ISO container next to us in which to keep drugs. Instead of the usual morning sick parade I would drive round the island in my Land Rover accompanied by Senior Aircraftsman (SAC) Briggs, my SEN, visiting the various encampments and units scattered about the place. We drove along a notified route to an approximate timetable and people would stand by the side of the road and wave us down if they wanted to consult us. It was the medical equivalent of the "Stop Me and Buy One" beloved of seaside ice cream salesmen.

To enliven proceedings as we drove round every day, SAC Briggs and I developed a game. At the top of the steepest hill, the Land Rover would be started moving, then put out of gear. Whoever was driving – we took it turn about – then tried to beat the previous record for freewheeling distance. It got more exciting as time went on and we had to keep going faster to go further, but we never had any mishaps. At the time I left SAC Briggs was winning.

A significant part of my job was dealing with the VC10 aeromedical evacuation flights which staged through the island on the way from the Falklands to UK. Very shortly after my arrival on Ascension my first one was due, and I received a message from the approaching aircraft that I should "definitely meet it on landing". Somewhat testily I replied that that was what I was there to do. Back came a reply that "I really should meet it". I feared the worst, and so it was. The first patient off the aircraft was an elderly Falkland Islander who was in a coma and clearly dying; she died about fifteen minutes after landing. I was upset not only for her, but for my reputation – doctors don't like losing patients, especially so soon after they've arrived. I telephoned the Administrator's office to report the death, and somewhat peremptorily said that I wanted to insist on a post-mortem examination. "Yes, that's fine; carry on," came the reply. I hung up, then started to wonder how it was to be achieved. It slowly dawned on me that it was probably down to me. That was a useful early reminder of how much we were on our own in the middle of the Atlantic. With the help of a good textbook Robin Whitla and I carried out the post-mortem, and I was professionally satisfied to produce findings which showed that the poor lady had really never had any chance. It might have been better if she had remained in the Falklands to die with her family around her.

Because I was required to be at the airfield for all RAF aircraft movements, under normal circumstances I could never go flying. However, one day I noticed from the flying programme that the last flight out was at 1000 and the next flight in wasn't due until just after 1300. I persuaded the Royal Navy helicopter flight, who had some Wessex aircraft for logistic support tasks, to take me up on an aerial tour of the island and its surrounding sea for an hour or so in the late morning. We were about as far away from the airfield as we were going when we heard a radio call from the last aircraft out that it had engine problems, had turned back and would be coming in to land shortly. Normally, under such circumstances, the helicopter would have kept out of the way while the airfield handled the emergency. But of course I needed to be on the airfield. We called up, explained the position, and I was down a few minutes before the returning aircraft landed – safely. In the excitement of it all no one noticed that I'd been doing what I shouldn't have been.

The working hours were long, but were seldom very busy. People did all sorts of things to fill in the time. One group of technicians had built a "fort", assembled from old packing cases and suitably painted, round their loo. SAC Briggs created a small "garden" outside our caravan with edging stones, cactuses and a sign saying "Keep off the Grass" (of which the nearest was about 800 miles away). I was appointed the services' representative to the island's Historical Society. We met weekly to discuss progress on identifying and finding the history of various artefacts people would hand in. A group of RAF technicians had restored an old 19th century fire truck. When this was presented to the island museum it was marked with a brass plaque recording the event, which described members of the historical society (including myself) as "Historians". Fame indeed!

Evening entertainment included turtle watching. A large number of Green Turtles would return to the island and the beach where they had been born to lay their eggs. You had to keep an appropriate distance away from them; but watching these huge creatures drag themselves up the beach, laboriously dig a hole with their flippers, lay their eggs and then cover them over was a fascinating sight – especially on a tropical beach by moonlight. The turtles headed back to the sea as soon as they had finished and were gone by morning.

The USAF had an open-air cinema to which all were welcome, but I seldom saw a film through to the end, as I was frequently called to see a patient from Africa. Each evening a Hercules aircraft would fly in from Dakar in Senegal, where we had a staging post, bringing urgent supplies. The small RAF contingent there had a French doctor to look after them, but they didn't seem to trust him. He was probably, like many French doctors, too keen on *le suppositoire*. So people would hitch a lift on the Hercules, see me while it was unloading, and return to Dakar with the aircraft. It's the only time patients have made a return journey of 3000 miles just to consult me.

From time to time a troopship making its way home from the Falklands would call in. My normal procedure was to contact the ship's surgeon and invite him to visit us while they were at anchor. They were usually glad to get ashore for a few hours and tour the sights. In return I would usually get invited back on board to dine with them. These tended to be very merry evenings, and I was always very grateful to the naval rating who ferried us safely to, and especially from, the ship.

Keeping in touch with home was an essential morale booster. Everyone was entitled to send an airmail letter (a "bluey") home free of charge each day; and there were no postal charges for blueys sent from UK to Ascension. In early February a tabloid newspaper sent a batch of Valentine's Day cards to the island so that every serviceman had a chance to send one home. They weren't perhaps in the best possible taste, but at least we had them; and Vivien still remembers it. Postal services for RAF Ascension were provided by the Royal Engineers postal and courier section, in our case in the form of a Staff Sergeant known to all as "Postie". His tent was next to our caravan, and as he was on his own we "adopted" him. One great benefit of doing so was that, when mail arrived, we got ours first.

Probably because of the frenetic way in which the Falklands Task Force had been kitted out, there was a lot of surplus equipment scattered about the island. SAC Briggs and I would occasionally stop on our rounds and look in an apparently unexplained lone tent to find out what was inside. In one we found hundreds of rifles. Leaving weapons unsecured and unguarded was virtually a hanging offence. I decided that the best way forward was for SAC Briggs, once we got back to the airfield, to go to talk to a mate of his who worked in the armoury. By next day the rifles had all gone.

Shortly after I arrived I had asked Sergeant Joe Jawaheer, my senior NCO Medical Assistant, if he could find me a typewriter. One duly appeared the next day. However we were now at a stage where various units in UK were looking to get their loaned equipment back again. A sergeant clerk from RAF Kinloss appeared in our caravan one day with a list of equipment they had sent to the war. Included on it was a typewriter. He spotted ours, and announced that it was one of the items on his list. We assured him it wasn't, and asked him to check the serial number; that had (perhaps unsurprisingly) disappeared. Only slightly put off by the lack of serial number, he looked at it some more and announced that he knew it was from RAF Kinloss. It had in fact been his own typewriter; to support his claim he told us that the crossbar of the lower case "e" was broken. Alas, this was true. I found an excuse to leave, so that the two sergeants could sort it out between them. A compromise was reached: we kept the typewriter until we could get a replacement, but we did admit it belonged to RAF Kinloss.

There were puzzles with more expensive items, too. On Christmas night, a serviceman had rolled a Land Rover on the hill coming down from Two Boats village to Georgetown. Neither he nor the vehicle was too badly damaged, and the possibility of alcohol intake was never actively pursued. However, come New Year's Eve, the Commander British Forces, Group Captain Roger Parker, ordered that all service vehicles had to be in the vehicle park by 2000, with the exception of a police vehicle to enforce the order, my Land Rover ambulance, a fire vehicle, and a coach which would drive on a continuous shuttle route round the island to transport those who wanted to move. A new Officer Commanding Engineering Wing had recently arrived on Ascension, and as part of his handover/takeover, he had signed for 128 "prime movers" – vehicles which can move under their own power. On New Year's Eve four of them were going about their business on the island. He therefore expected to find 124 in the vehicle park. There were 137. It got sorted out eventually.

The Officers' Mess at RAF Lyneham had commissioned the aviation artist Penelope Douglas to produce a painting of a VC10 at Ascension during an aeromedevac turn round. She was a cousin of Group Captain Tony Balfour, the RAF's senior aviation pathologist, which is probably why I was given the job of helping her liaise with all those around the station whom she needed to facilitate her work. It was great fun, and almost everyone joined in with great gusto. On the day we had a scene set up just as she wanted for her to sketch and photograph. In the finished painting I can clearly identify myself, standing beside the ambulance and looking suitably officious.

At the beginning of my last week on Ascension we received a call from the MV *Leopold-LD*, a French cargo ship then in the middle of the South Atlantic. She had on board a seaman with what was described as "digestive bleeding" and was seeking help in having him evacuated to the nearest medical facility; which meant us. The Naval Wessex helicopters which we would have to use to pick him up, whose war role was transporting Marines ashore or about the battlefield, didn't have the sophisticated navigation equipment you really should have for going significant distances across the South Atlantic so we planned to have a Hercules giving us top cover and navigational assistance. We had to wait until the ship was sufficiently near for us to reach her within the Wessex's fuel limits; but even so, when we got there I knew I had only five minutes to decide whether to take the casualty immediately, or stay to resuscitate and stabilise him while the helicopter returned to Ascension, refuelled, and came back to get us.

My experience of SAR and casevac at RAF Valley and in Hong Kong had led me to be highly suspicious about the descriptions of patients' problems which were passed to me. I was right to be so. The full story was that the seaman, an alcoholic, had been locked in his cabin to keep him away from the booze. He had escaped, and in the ensuing chase round the ship he had tripped and fallen into one of the holds. When I was taken into his cabin, he was lying on his bunk, dead.

Then he groaned, and I realised that he only looked dead. The Master of the *Leopold* had rigged up a rectal drip – "intravenous" fluid put into you via your rectum, which, though not ideal, had probably saved the man's life. He had a very low blood pressure and a slow pulse, a compound fracture of his left upper arm, with a bit of obviously dead and probably infected bone sticking out, head injuries and bruising, and an abdomen which, on examination, gave indications that in addition he probably did have the "digestive bleeding" which we had been told about to start with. His situation was critical. I decided to take him off straight away, as the extra two hours or so before we got him to hospital might well have been the end of him.

Back at Ascension, Robin, Raj and the hospital team were waiting for us. We got him rehydrated and stabilised before taking him to the operating theatre where, while Robin gassed him, I assisted Raj in cutting away all the dead and infected tissue and bone, cleaning up his injuries and dealing with what turned out in the end to be a very mild internal bleed.

He made a good recovery, but clearly needed a lot more definitive surgery to get him properly sorted out. He was well enough to travel back to UK on the next aeromedevac, on which I accompanied him at the end of my tour. After the rest of the team had taken him off to the RAF hospital at Wroughton, I looked around for the staff car which had been arranged to take me back to Cranwell. No one seemed to know anything about it. I was just about to make a short, sharp telephone call when round the corner came Vivien and the children (and the dog) who had come to welcome me and take me home. It made for a very happy ending to a varied and offbeat couple of months.

7

Resting Hawk

The role of the Royal Air Force Staff College at Bracknell was to train suitable officers for the most senior appointments in the service. To get there was of itself a recognition that, so far, you were succeeding in your RAF career. The College badge was a Hawk, signifying the Egyptian god Horus, who was variously described as the god of the sky and of war. It had its eyes closed and its wings folded, symbolising, as Air Vice-Marshal Tony Skingsley, the commandant, told us in his welcome lecture, warriors taking a rest from their duties to contemplate and consider the future. The motto was *Visu et Nisu* – By Vision and Effort. Quite how you achieved the former with your eyes closed was never explained.

There was certainly a lot of effort. The previous year's course, during the end of course debrief, had commented – I think "complained" would be putting it too strongly – that they didn't feel they had been worked very hard. The system took this on board and racked things up accordingly for us. However it undoubtedly was a break from hard work at the front line. It took me a little time to adjust from being on call every second or third night and weekend. Occasionally in the evening I would hear an aircraft pass over on its way to or from Heathrow and for a brief moment I would wonder which medical officer was covering night flying.

There were ninety of us on the course. The majority were from the RAF, but we had twenty-four students from overseas, two from the Royal Navy, three from the Army, one Royal Marine and two MOD civil servants. It was an interesting mixture and made for a wide range of views. We were a competitive group; opportunities to show off your enthusiasm and greater knowledge and judgement were seldom passed over; but it was all (mostly) good-natured. Over the years I had come across a certain type of pilot, fortunately small in number, who took the view that, because I was a doctor, I couldn't (not didn't, but *couldn't*) know anything about air power or technical matters. There were a couple of them on the course, and it was a source of great satisfaction to me to show them otherwise – especially if I could win them over to my view during discussions.

Lectures were held in the Brooke-Popham lecture theatre, named after Air Chief Marshal Sir Robert Brooke-Popham, the first commandant of the RAF Staff College. We had an excellent range of speakers over the year, but inevitably some were more stimulating than others. Not for nothing was it sometimes referred to as "Bedroom 1". As the years pass, I find that the lectures I remember most were from those who strayed a little from their advertised or expected script.

We were an all-male course. When Len Murray, then General Secretary of the TUC, finished his lecture he said, "Well, brothers, it has been a pleasure to talk to you. But no sisters? You should be ashamed." General Sir Michael Gow, whose lecture was intended to sum up part of the course with a title something like "Whither the Armoured Battlefield?" instead gave a thought-provoking talk on the ethics and morals of killing people, which is ultimately what the armed forces are for.

We worked on our various tasks in syndicates of seven, with one of the directing staff (DS) as leader. We studied doctrine and strategy, the principles of war, uses of air power, command and control, advances in technology and communication skills. We looked at the structure of society and how various parts of it worked. We wrote plans, briefs, appreciations, minutes, papers, operation orders and all manner of staff paperwork. Increasingly we looked at joint operations with the other two services – "jointery" had been one of the big lessons of the Falklands War the year before. We had joint sessions with the Army and Navy Staff Colleges. During these the tendency to try to impress fellow students and the DS was amplified almost to the level of caricature.

On the Army Staff course was Major Ken Millar RAMC, who had been my exact contemporary at school and at university. Our careers followed parallel paths after staff college, and with that and the fact that we both sent our children to Fettes I continued to see a lot of him throughout my service career. There was a joint Army/ RAF session on St Andrew's day, and at lunch Ken and I celebrated in style with some excellent claret. Our memory of the afternoon programme is rather hazy.

Fortunately, it wasn't all talk and paperwork. We had a lot of visits to the military in the field and to civilian organisations. We visited the Army in Germany, exploring how they and our allies were planning to cope with Russian hordes expected one day to charge towards them across the north German plain. On our final day there, the German Army gave us an alfresco lunch in a clearing somewhere in the Harz Mountains. At the end of it Tony Skingsley, who spoke fluent German, rose and gave a marvellously witty speech of thanks which had even the waiters rolling about laughing. Just as he finished, a pair of RAF Jaguars flew low across the clearing. This was a complete coincidence, but our hosts were very impressed.

During Navy Week we visited a number of their shore establishments and "fought" a sea battle on their Tactical Training Floor at Midhurst in Hampshire. The highlight of the week was our day at sea, where we were split among a number of warships who carried out a short demonstration exercise in the Channel. I got my first choice of vessel, an SSK ("hunter-killer") submarine. I had seen numerous war films involving submarines, and the scene inside ours showed that they were remarkably true to life. Everything was very cramped, and all personnel squeezed themselves out of the way as the captain strode past. I had one disappointment, though. In the films, at the command "Up Periscope", the captain turns his hat round so that the peak is at the back while he applies his eye to the lens. In the real world they don't wear hats, so he can't.

We were hunted ourselves by the ships on the surface. When our hunter's sonar caught us it "pinged" within the submarine. I had heard this in the films, and had assumed it didn't really happen but was added to the soundtrack for heightened drama. Hearing it for real in a small cramped metal tube under water, even when you know it's only an exercise, puts your pulse rate up quite a bit. My admiration for submariners was even greater after that day.

The Navy hosted a tri-service Staff College dinner in the Painted Hall at Greenwich. It was a splendid evening in wonderful surroundings. At one point I turned to the Italian Army officer sitting on my left and commented on the magnificent ceiling. He glanced at it briefly, shrugged his shoulders and said, "We have two just like this in my home town". 2–1 to Italy.

One of the social highlights of the year at Bracknell was International Night. Each of the overseas students organised a stall illustrating their country's history and culture and provided samples of typical food and drink. Members of their Embassies and High Commissions were invited along. All the stalls were impressive – there was a great deal of competition involved. The Saudi Arabian stall was outstanding. It was erected and manned by a team which clearly did this, anywhere and as required, as a full-time job. We were slightly disappointed they hadn't brought a camel.

I decided that there should be a Scotland stall. I got a selection of stuff from the Scottish Tourist Board, bought some haggis, and persuaded an old school friend, whom I had met a few weeks earlier at an Old Fettesian drinks party in London and who was now director of a whisky firm, to provide me with a (more than) adequate number of bottles. It went down very well. As the evening wore on, Major Mohammed al-Amri from the Sultan of Oman's Air Force came for his fourth "sample" of the water of life.

"Mo, I thought you Muslims didn't drink whisky."

"Iain, I am a good Muslim. I only drink good whisky."

Sadly, Mo was killed in a flying accident in Oman a few years later.

We were encouraged to play sport, and at one point there was an inter-syndicate rugby sevens competition. As each syndicate only had seven members, selection was automatic. I hadn't played rugby properly since leaving school, and not at all for about fifteen years. At the end of our only match – fortunately we were knocked out in the first round – I could hardly stand. I had cycled down to the sports pitches, but couldn't cycle back. Instead, my bicycle served as a Zimmer frame. Never again.

Bracknell had a number of Guns in the Army Staff College shoot, and I was lucky to have one of these. Another of the RAF Guns was David Felwick, who had left the RAF the previous year and who for his last tour had been on the DS at Bracknell. He had joined the John Lewis Partnership as a Senior Management Trainee, and as we walked through the Surrey countryside he waxed lyrical about the Partnership and what it offered. I was to remember him and his words some years later when I was contemplating leaving.

We had a proper long summer break. Many of the overseas students used it to travel round the UK and Europe. Lieutenant Colonel Peter Atambo from Kenya planned to drive all round Britain. His wife Yvonne was joining him from Kenya for the summer. Peter, a very impressive man, had been President Jomo Kenyatta's personal pilot. He spoke perfect English, with a distinct received pronunciation accent. We were spending the summer at our cottage in the Scottish Borders, and we arranged for the Atambos to call in for lunch on the day they would be passing us. I supplied a full brief on how to find us, with routes, map references and the rest. They were due with us at one o'clock, but didn't arrive until quarter past two. Peter had forgotten to bring my brief with him (you can imagine how sympathetic Yvonne was), but had dealt with the situation as he told me he would have done in Kenya. He had vaguely remembered the area where we were and that we were "about an hour south-east of Edinburgh". So he drove down the most south-east pointing road for an hour, then got out and started asking people where the McCoubreys lived. Astonishingly, it worked. Back in 1983 the average border small farmer wasn't used to a large and imposing black man dropping in unexpectedly and speaking perfect English. Some of our neighbours were still talking about him years later.

When we visited the RAF in Germany, we had our "own" VC10 to take us about. After visiting the headquarters at Rheindalen, and one of the flying stations nearby, we headed off to Berlin. It was still technically under four-power (USA, USSR, UK and France) military government. The British Military Governor, Major General David Mostyn, welcomed us with a presentation about the city. It opened with a seven-minute film taken by a reconnaissance aircraft flying over the city in 1945. For the full seven minutes all we saw were bombed, shelled and burnt-out buildings. When it had finished, he asked us to compare what we had just seen with what we had seen when we had flown in ourselves a few hours earlier. The changes over the thirty-eight years were spectacular. General Mostyn then asked us to consider whether Berlin would still be as it was today in a further thirty-eight years; or in twenty years? Or ten? Or maybe fifty? We all agreed that the current situation couldn't go on for ever; but I don't think anyone reckoned that it would take only another six years for the Berlin wall to fall and the USSR to start to disintegrate.

We toured East Berlin. The difference between the two halves was of course marked, but there was one feature present on both sides of the wall: parking spaces marked "For Allied Use Only". A real privilege! Another of the leftovers from the end of WWII was the Berlin Air Safety Centre. Civil aircraft all over Germany were controlled by the international Air Traffic Control system. Military flights to and from Berlin from the West were authorised by this group of four officers, one from each of the occupying powers. It was undoubtedly outdated, but no one wanted to do away with anything in the post-war four-power agreements for fear that the whole edifice would collapse. Despite it being the middle of the cold war, the three Western allies got on well with their Russian counterpart at least on a personal working level. However, the Russian, when he signed the document approving a flight, always applied a rubber stamp stating that "The safety of this flight cannot be guaranteed."

On the last night in Berlin we all went out on the town. Coming home with a couple of friends in the early morning we spotted a van selling bratwurst and chips – what British servicemen referred to as a "Brattie Wagon". This, we decided, would hit the spot, so we joined a small queue. In front of us was a very drunk German who, having been served, turned away, tripped, fell his length and scattered his brattie and chips all over the road. He got up, very angry, and began to upbraid the brattie man, demanding that he be supplied free with another helping. The brattie man would have none of it and finally sought to bring him under control by telling him that he was "making a fool of himself in front of some Allied officers". We were rather delighted to see the effect this produced. The drunk quietened down and shambled off.

Next morning we were all sitting in the foyer of Edinburgh House, the British service accommodation in Berlin, waiting for the bus to take us to the airfield. Many of us were rather the worse for wear. I was reading Jane Austen (in a hardback edition – a paperback would not have had sufficient gravitas). On being asked what I was reading, I was able to answer, "*Sense and Sensibility* – of which I have seen very little over the past twenty-four hours." It was the sort of posing we all did, so all I got was groans rather than being thumped for being pretentious.

We flew down the military air corridor at 10,000 feet – the

maximum height, as when it was set up in 1945 that was as high as aircraft were expected to go. When we were handed over to civilian air traffic control in West Germany, they allowed us to continue at 10,000 feet all the way home. It was a clear day, and we had a panoramic view of Northern Europe and Southern England as we made our way back to RAF Brize Norton.

During the course we all had to write a dissertation – the "Brooke-Popham Essay". Although you could choose your own subject, it had to be approved by the DS, as all the completed essays would be circulated among the relevant staffs at MOD. A cynic might argue that it was a cheap way to get a number of feasibility studies carried out. My subject was "Should we privatise the RAF Hospitals in the UK?" The thesis was in essence that it might be cheaper to take out a mass subscription to BUPA rather than run our own hospitals. But I needed to show how, if we did so, we could still carry out our various wartime commitments. Having thoroughly researched the subject over the year, I put forward the pros and cons, and concluded that actually we shouldn't privatise the hospitals – not least because once they'd got the contract and we'd closed our hospitals, the private medical care providers would have us over a barrel.

I was quite pleased with it, and the DS were satisfied. It was sent for review to the headquarters of RAF Support Command, which controlled all the RAF hospitals in the UK. Shortly afterwards I received a phone call from a somewhat irritated Air Vice-Marshal Dick Riseley-Pritchard, the Principal Medical Officer at the headquarters. What did I think I was doing, exploring a sensitive subject like this? I protested that, having explored the subject and examined the evidence, I had recommended against it. "Yes," he said, "but if you tear off the back page with the recommendations, you've done all the work for Heseltine (Michael, then Defence Secretary) to close us down." This wasn't quite the case, but it contained more than a grain of truth. "The Director General will have to see this," thundered Dick in conclusion. This was not good.

I had just been told I was to be posted to the Director General's staff after the course.

The final night was celebrated with a grand dinner, attended by all the great and good of the RAF from the Chief of Air Staff down. The after-dinner entertainment was a revue put on by the students. I had been given the job of organising it, and had to put together a varied programme which would not only gently mock what we had been through, and of course be full of in-jokes, but also entertain our guests. As well as a selection of sketches, we had a video tape of farewell messages to the course given by many of our visiting lecturers recorded immediately after they had spoken to us. Lieutenant Colonel Bob Vollenweider, our Swiss officer, was a keen choral singer and had organised a choir of overseas students to sing 'Maybe it's Because I'm a Londoner'. A pop group consisting of four of the wives (including Vivien), dressed in RAF shirts, high heels and not a lot else, went down very well, especially with our senior guests. And of course we finished with all the cast on stage, leading the audience in singing 'Auld Lang Syne'. Then it was back to the real world.

8

Chief Paperkeeper

One day during my time as SMO at Cranwell, when Flight Sergeant Hibberd, my senior NCO Medical Assistant, brought me in the morning's mail and files, he had on the top of the pile a Defence Council Instruction, the official gazette of the MOD, in which was advertised the post of Chief Paperkeeper, somewhere in the organisation. He pointed it out with glee. Senior NCOs tend to have a very low opinion of the MOD and all its works; that such a job existed served pointedly to reinforce his opinion that nothing good could ever come from it.

I hoped I wasn't about to be a disappointment to him. The job in MOD to which I was posted involved, among other things, being custodian of all medical officers' annual confidential reports. I would be keeping a great deal of paper.

My post's official title was Medical Administration 1 (RAF). No one ever called it anything but MA1; but that didn't tell you much about it either. I was on the staff of the Director General of RAF Medical Services (always known, even sometimes to his face, as "the DG") and was responsible for personnel matters for RAF medical officers. This included recruiting, training, career progression, disciplinary matters and manning. I wouldn't be practising any medicine, and wouldn't be involved with any flying. On the other hand, it would give me a unique insight into the people who made the RAF medical services work. If you were at all ambitious, it would not have escaped your notice that virtually all those who became the DG had at one time been MA1. It was definitely what was known as a career posting.

My arrival interview with the DG, Air Marshal Sir David Atkinson (who had been MA1 himself some twenty years previously), confirmed my thoughts about the job. "When you leave," he said, "you will know more about more people than you would have believed possible. And you will find that information very useful for the rest of your career." It was a very pleasant interview. There was no mention of my Brooke-Popham essay, which Dick Riseley-Pritchard had assured me the DG would have to see. I was greatly relieved. At my next interview, with the deputy DG, Air Commodore Mike Rogers, all was revealed. At some point in what was another pleasant interview he said, "Oh, by the way, you should be aware that Dick Riseley-Pritchard sent up your staff college paper for the DG to see. He was quite aerated about it; too much, in my opinion. I decided the DG didn't need to see it." Mike Rogers was clearly a man of sound judgement.

I had been promoted to Wing Commander on appointment to the post, and we were living in RAF married quarters in Bushey Heath, in Hertfordshire. I had a one-hour commute into work on the tube every morning, and the same home in the evening. It was very different. And it takes time to adjust.

We are all creatures of habit, and old habits die hard. I had to do a lot of interviewing; people who had expressed an interest in a career in the RAF; applicants for cadetships or commissions; and serving RAF medical officers who, for various reasons, requested or required an interview. After over sixteen years of clinical work, it took me about three weeks before I realised that I didn't, in the absence of a washbasin in my office, have to go down to the loo and wash my hands between patients – or rather, interviewees.

I had a week's handover with my predecessor, Wing Commander

Pat Hickey. He was a fervent coffee drinker, refilling his cup almost as soon as he emptied it. As the new boy, I kept pace with him for the first morning, but by that afternoon was almost twitching as a result of caffeine overdose. I took coffee at my own rate after that. Pat was an outstanding medical officer and a fitness fanatic. It was a shock to all and a great loss to the service when, a few years later, he had a stroke and was invalided out.

Manning was the biggest problem in the job. We were chronically short of medical officers. It was virtually standard practice to have a gap of two weeks between one junior MO leaving a post and his or her successor arriving. Do that twenty-six times, and you have saved yourself a man-year. Planning to fill anticipated vacancies was always at risk of being rendered nugatory by "the exigencies of the service" – that is, the need to meet sudden and often unexpected operational demands. Keeping numbers up required not just recruiting but also retention. One of my stronger cards for the latter was to offer the more desirable postings to those who were prepared to extend their service.

I had another bribe up my sleeve in the form of the Flight Medical Officers' (FMO's) flying course. This offered forty hours of flying training to appropriately qualified officers, and entitled those who successfully completed it to wear the FMO's flying badge. It was a very useful tool for persuading people they really wanted to go to an unpopular job. One FMO's flying course greatly helped at both ends of the manning challenge. Squadron Leader Josephine Kingston, on beginning the course, became the first woman ever to receive RAF pilot training. We got a great deal of publicity out of it, and a noticeable uptake in female applicants for cadetships.

Prospective cadets were assessed at the Officers and Aircrew Selection Centre at RAF Biggin Hill, and medical cadets were then further assessed by me at a professional interview. One young woman arrived from Biggin Hill with excellent assessments. During my interview it became clear that she was exceedingly keen to gain a cadetship. Her cause was in no way diminished by one of her referees being Flight Lieutenant Hector Skinner, who, although she didn't know it, had been my first ever flying instructor. She had done all sorts of things to impress us and I wanted to congratulate her on her efforts. I said, "You're prepared to do anything to get this, aren't you?" As it came out I realised that, phrased that way, it was capable of being misinterpreted. She didn't seem to notice, but I hurried the interview to a close. I immediately went to my two female clerical assistants (CAs) and told them what had happened, to begin to build some sort of defence when a formal complaint came whizzing through the door. My CAs laughed uproariously and said they expected it was merely the effect of the large amount of scent she had been wearing. No complaint arrived. Some years later I met the lady, by then a Squadron Leader, and raised the subject of the interview. She assured me that the possible *double entendre* had never entered her mind.

Halfway through my tour I was accepted to appear on the TV quiz *Mastermind*. My specialist subject was "The History of Hong Kong". Although the programme looks tense and terrifying, filming it was great fun. The only sad bit was that my programme was recorded at St Bartholomew's Hospital, which was just down the road from my office; so I didn't get the all-expenses-paid trip away that I might have had, although there was an excellent post-recording party. I did fairly well, but didn't get through to the next round. My disappointment was tempered by the knowledge that I wouldn't have to spend the next three months living and breathing my second subject – the "Alms for Oblivion" novels of Simon Raven. I had got really fed up with the history of Hong Kong.

Just across the road from our offices in High Holborn was a building which housed part of the meteorological office. The BBC weather forecast was sometimes broadcast from a room on the ground floor which had a large plate-glass window so that passers-by could watch Ian McCaskill or whoever doing their stuff. Out of my office window I could see the roof of their building, on which was a collection of meteorological instruments from which they drew some of their data. One day I couldn't see the roof of their building, because the rain was falling so heavily that visibility was only about 50 yards. At the same time I had a radio on to get the lunchtime news. It was preceded by the weather forecast, which included the words "In London it's a fine day". I've never really trusted the BBC weather forecast since.

People had been practising occupational medicine, which concerns itself with the effects of work on health and the effects of health on work, since at least the 17th century, when an Italian called Ramazzini had taken an interest in what his patients did for a living. The first person to write about it in the UK was Charles Thackrah, who practised in Leeds at the beginning of the 19th century. During the 1970s there had been a move to recognise it as a specific discipline, and the Royal College of Physicians had formed a Faculty of Occupational Medicine. Membership of this Faculty was to become a prerequisite for being recognised as a specialist and appointed a consultant. Of course there was a "grandfather clause", allowing those with sufficient knowledge, qualifications and experience to be granted Membership without having to sit the exam. There was also a limited time for those who *almost* met the criteria to gain further qualifications or experience and thus also avoid the exam. I had fallen into the latter category, and had been told that I needed more experience. My time in Hong Kong and Cranwell counted but, according to their published criteria, I was still short of sufficient valid experience. A year at Staff College and three years as a personnel officer were not going to add anything, and time was running out. I submitted an application at the last minute, making much of the fact that I was spending four years out of occupational medicine purely to serve Queen and Country, and with an assurance from my boss that after this tour I would be moving to a post fully engaged in occupational medicine. It worked. They granted me Membership (so I would avoid the exam. Hooray!) but withheld recognition as a specialist until I had completed the couple of months' experience still prescribed. Their letter came on my thirty-eighth birthday; it was an excellent present.

As Sir David Atkinson had indicated, I learned a lot, but it was not just about people. In particular, there were three aphorisms which I had heard bandied about over the years whose basic soundness was firmly brought home to me during my time at MA1.

The first was that "Rules are for the obedience of fools and the guidance of wise men". There was a mountain of rules covering everything I had to do in minute detail. If I'd followed every one of them to the letter, nothing would ever have been done (Flight Sergeant Hibbert was right, you see). So I did whatever seemed to me to be sensible under the circumstances. As time passed I got braver – and braver. They haven't caught up with me yet.

Then there's "No solution equals no problem". At first I would get quite unhappy when, unable to meet everyone's demands because I didn't have the resources, assorted people would berate me and cast aspersions about my competence. As time passed I realised that, if there really wasn't a solution – and sometimes there just wasn't – then worrying about it helped nobody and got us nowhere. I was acutely aware that the psychiatrists were prone to label such behaviour *la belle indifférence* and an indication of mental health problems. But I decided it didn't apply to me.

The third of the trio probably came from Disraeli but was popularised by Mark Twain. "There are lies, damned lies and statistics." I was regularly required to produce statistics about manning and the like. In the days before computers it involved quite a lot of work. One of the most common questions I was asked was, "What is the size of the RAF medical services?" To give the best answer, you needed to know the context of the question, who was asking it and why. You then made a decision about which answer would best meet your aims. If you wanted to appear small (and therefore less costly than others, for example) the number supplied included only fully registered medical officers actually working in service posts at that time. If you wanted to appear large (and therefore not suitable for being amalgamated with something else, for example) the number offered would include all medical officers and cadets, all dental officers and cadets, all nursing officers and all medical support officers. No one ever queried my figures. I suspect that the vast majority of my questioners didn't really know what they were asking about.

The biggest misuse of statistics of all was after a tri-service study and report, which amalgamated the headquarters of all three services' medical people into one organisation. There was of course downsizing, reduction in ranks and many other uncomfortable changes. But at the end, there were still a number of tri-service posts to be filled. My immediate boss had a meeting one day with his opposite numbers from the Navy and Army to horse-trade and to allocate the posts to each service. I sat in a back room providing figures to back our arguments. I hesitate to call them statistics. The most ridiculous set of figures I produced involved the use of "ratios of percentages", a concept I had just invented, and which were of no statistical value whatever. But they got us the jobs we wanted. Very occasionally I worry that this sort of thing goes on everywhere and, as with us, goes undetected.

And of course I learned that *Yes Minister* is in fact a documentary.

To support my application for Membership of the Faculty of Occupational Medicine my boss had stated that I would move on to a post fully engaged with occupational medicine. This was absolutely true. One of the perks of being MA1 was that, at the end of your tour you got to choose (within reason) where you would go next. I chose to be the Command Flight Medical Officer, the aviation medicine man at Headquarters Strike Command, the operational end of the Royal Air Force.

9

Strike Command

The quaintly named village of Walters Ash, set in the leafy beech woods above High Wycombe, was the unlikely location for the headquarters of RAF Strike Command. It controlled the sharp end of the air force – all the operational stations in the UK as well as a number of overseas locations such as Cyprus, Hong Kong and Gibraltar. The accommodation was originally built as a headquarters for Bomber Command in WWII, and now houses the headquarters of Air Command. I arrived there on the 15th of September – Battle of Britain Day – 1986. My job, reporting to the Principal Medical Officer (PMO) Air Vice-Marshal Eddie Simpson, was to provide aviation medicine advice to the headquarters staff and consultant cover to the SMOs on the many stations which made up the command. By now I had fulfilled the remaining experience requirements and had been appointed a consultant in occupational medicine to the RAF.

The most unpredictable and dramatic aspect of the job was aircraft accident investigation. Despite all possible precautions, from time to time we would lose an aircraft – and sometimes the aircrew as well. Whenever there was an accident a board of enquiry would be set up, and a team, of which I was part, would go out to investigate. On the medical side there would be input from me, from the IAM at Farnborough, and from the aviation pathology department of the RAF's Institute of Pathology. Speed was of the essence. It was reckoned that about fifty per cent of the relevant evidence would be lost within twenty-four hours. From a human factors point of view, I needed to interview surviving aircrew as soon as possible. With the passage of time, especially after a life-changing event such as a crash or ejection, your brain starts to rationalise what "must" have happened rather than remember what actually did happen. As well as looking for possible medical causes for the accident – physical and psychological (such as one of the many illusions to which aircrew are subject in the unnatural environment of flying) and looking at injuries, we needed to find out whether the ejection system had worked properly and protected the aircrew as it should. Production of a final detailed report would take months, but there was always pressure from the top to advise if there was any immediately obvious problem with the aircraft or its equipment which might indicate that all similar aircraft should be grounded pending further investigation.

If there had been a fatality, it could be a pretty gruesome process. On the other hand hunting round the crash site for clues – photographing everything for the record and where possible leaving everything in place – also made it fascinating. Surviving aircrew's stories could be strangely amusing. One pilot, who finished up hanging from his parachute in a tree after ejecting at about 500 feet, described squeezing his harness release box and it not opening until the second time he tried. I seized on this. Had there been a malfunction of the release box? The pilot thought not. It was just that, having ejected and then found himself hanging from a tree, he hadn't really squeezed it properly since he wasn't sure he wanted another bit of involuntary falling that day. Tests on the release box showed it in perfect working order.

Another pilot, having been involved in a mid-air collision, found himself upside down, out of control, and heading downwards very close to the ground. He was obviously going to die. But his training told him to eject, so he did so, accepting that he would probably tent-peg himself into the ground. To his very great surprise, at that moment he passed over an 800 foot escarpment, which gave enough height above ground for his parachute to open and for him to descend safely.

We would seek out and talk to anyone in the area who might have seen the accident happening. On one occasion in Norfolk, a farmer had been out checking his stock when an aircraft, obviously in difficulties, flew past him and crashed in a field. He noticed which hills had obscured it and which it had cleared, dug out an ordnance survey map and his old trigonometry book, and calculated the height of the aircraft when he saw it. When we got the black box flight recorder, we found that his answer was remarkably accurate.

More than once, walking back to the road down a farm track after several hours scouring a hillside, we were invited into a farmhouse or cottage for a cup of tea; although I suspect that a chance to get the latest information was as much a motivation as kindness.

Once while being driven to an accident in mid-Wales in an RAF staff car, together with aviation pathologist Group Captain Tony Balfour and an engineering officer, we passed GCHQ in Cheltenham. We didn't talk about the intelligence services in those days, and I was amused to note that we were all looking straight ahead and pretending we didn't know it was there.

When an accident report was finalised, it would be circulated round the headquarters for the relevant departments to add official comments. I did the medical part. I also provided input and comment on parachuting accidents. Although I understood what parachutists did, and the various stresses and strains which parachuting put on the human body, I had never jumped myself. I was aware that there was a one-jump course designed to give people like me the necessary experience so I phoned Squadron Leader Chris Abbott, a fellow medical officer who was himself a parachutist and well in with the parachute mafia, to ask his advice. He assured me that he would arrange it all for me. A little later I was told to report to the parachuting school at RAF Brize Norton for three days.

When I got there I found that I was joining the beginning of a free-fall parachuting course for the SAS. All the other course members, as well as being ludicrously fit, were already qualified military parachutists. None of them spoke to me for the first session. At the coffee break I explained who I was and why I was there. They then talked to me; they had assumed that I was to be "inserted" somewhere and so on the need-to-know principle weren't going to ask me anything.

The first day was ground training. On the second and third days we were scheduled to do a total of six jumps before the other members of the course set off to the USA to complete a month's training. On day two the weather was outside our limits, so we did some more ground training. Fortunately on day three the weather improved and I was able to make three jumps. After all the training I felt reasonably confident, if a little anxious. Reassuringly, we each had an individual instructor who stood in front of you and walked backwards out of the aircraft just before you jumped. He then "flew" in formation with you until you pulled the cord and the parachute opened. Better still, he made a video of you and took pictures. I still have them.

The parachutes we used were very controllable. You could fly them like an aircraft – or at least like an aircraft on a constant descent. The aim was to land as close as possible to a target on the airfield. You then picked up your parachute and ran at the double back to the bus – a distance of about half a mile. Jumps one and two went well, and I was pleased to hit the target both times. By jump three, my lack of fitness compared with the SAS lads was beginning to show. Besides, I thought, this is probably my last ever jump and there is a definite limit on what a Flight Sergeant – even a parachute jumping instructor – can do to a Wing Commander who doesn't do what he's told. So on my third jump I pulled the handle far too early and spent a lovely gentle five minutes floating down over the

Oxfordshire countryside. And I landed beside the bus, which saved me the run. The Flight Sergeant said, "Do you know, sir, I thought you might do something like that."

My father had been with SOE during WWII and had parachuted into Yugoslavia as an adviser to Tito's partisans. In homage to him, when jumping I wore the watch he had been given for the job. I was only sorry he wasn't still around for me to tell him about it.

At one stage in my tour I did a spell as deputy president of the mess (Strike Command being a large place full of senior people, the president had to be a Group Captain). When HRH Princess Alice, Duchess of Gloucester, Air Chief Commandant of the WRAF visited, the president was absent on duty so I took his place at the formal lunch in the mess. Our Commander-in-Chief, Air Chief Marshal Sir Peter Harding (who had been my station commander at Bruggen) was seated next to the duchess and I was next to her lady-in-waiting, Dame Jean Maxwell Scott.

As part of the preparations for the visit, those of us at the lunch had to submit a brief biography so that the Royal party would have some idea who they were to meet. Dame Jean was a direct descendant of Sir Walter Scott the novelist, and lived at Abbotsford, the house he built by the river Tweed near Melrose. Being aware of this I mentioned that I had grown up in the Scottish Borders, and had been to prep school in Melrose. We didn't move in the same circles, but I hoped that would give an opening for conversation. During the soup, Dame Jean chatted away and quite clearly was trying to place me. After a few minutes she suddenly said, "I know who you are – you're Dr McCoubrey's boy." I was forty-two at the time, but it was a very pleasing thing to be called twelve years after my father's death. Once again I was sorry he wasn't still around for me to tell him about it.

After the luncheon there was an official photograph of the Princess and her entourage, Sir Peter, Air Commodore Shirley Jones, Director of the WRAF and all the WRAF Officers at Strike

Command. Once it had been taken, Sir Peter made his excuses and went back to work, leaving me and Shirley Jones to say farewell to the Princess. As we stood outside the Mess saluting, a voice from inside hissed, "Iain, get back in here. One of the girls has passed out." As soon as the Princess' car had disappeared round the corner I ran in. A young WRAF Officer was slumped unconscious in an armchair. It was a hot day, she was in her best uniform, and she was perhaps slightly cuddlier than she had been when she was measured for the uniform.

I lifted her up, laid her flat on the floor, picked up her heels and handed them to someone to hold; unbuttoned her uniform jacket, unzipped and unbuttoned her skirt waistband, slipped a hand round the back and undid her bra; all in about five seconds. With gravity-assisted return of blood to her core and released from the constrictions of her clothing, the young lady came round almost immediately. I looked up, straight into the eyes of Shirley Jones. "You've done that before, Iain," she said pointedly. "Yes, ma'am," I replied, and grinned. She grinned back.

I was responsible for advice on medical aspects of search and rescue (SAR). Given my experiences at Valley and Hong Kong, this was a particular interest. We undertook a review of first aid training for SAR crewmen. It began on the 1st of May – Mayday! – an ideal time to start as our chairman noted. Early on in my tour, to refresh myself on how it all worked, I visited two SAR flights, at RAF Boulmer (flying Sea King aircraft) and RAF Leuchars (flying Wessex aircraft).

At Boulmer I found myself doing my last ever operational SAR sortie. We were in the air somewhere over Northumberland when we heard the sound of a distress beacon over the radio. As we headed towards the source we were told that a German Tornado aircraft had disappeared off the radar. We soon got to the site of a typical "flight into ground" accident, with aircraft parts spread in a line over the countryside, and a burning mass at the end. There was no sign of either of the crew having ejected. Fearing the worst,

I was put down to (cautiously) look round the wreckage. I had my camera with me and was able to get a number of photographs for the subsequent Luftwaffe board of enquiry. Unsurprisingly I soon came across first one then the other of the two aircrew, both dead. There was nothing more we could do, so having notified the exact position to the recovery team, which was already nearing the site, we headed for home. This had been my fiftieth SAR sortie. It was sad that it involved two deaths. The only "good" thing was that, both deceased having been first seen and then formally declared dead by a Registered Medical Practitioner, many of the administrative difficulties which might have arisen were avoided.

A Boulmer crew flew me up to Leuchars. At the time of my visit there was a NATO summit taking place at Gleneagles, and Leuchars was being used as the arrival point. As we flew in we could see that the station's air defence missiles had been boosted for the occasion. I had booked myself into the mess for a couple of days, but was delighted – and astonished, for he certainly had enough on his plate with NATO bigwigs coming and going through his station – when the station commander, Group Captain Ian Macfadyen, met me at the helicopter and took me off, announcing that I would be staying with him. Ian and I had been flight lieutenants together during my first tour at Cranwell; he had been a member of the "Poachers" aerobatic team. His career had flourished (and continued to do so). He had landed the first aircraft on the runway at Port Stanley after the Falklands War. He would later go on to be Chief of Staff to Sir Peter de la Billière during the first Gulf War in 1991, and much more. But this is my story, not his.

Ian and his wife Sally were excellent hosts. Of course, as in any working household, breakfast was functional. On day one it was cereal in the kitchen. During that day the Minister for the Armed Forces, Sir John Stanley, visited one of the squadrons at Leuchars on his way home from the NATO meeting. The squadron commander, Wing Commander Philip Roser, had been his Military Assistant and the Minister was dropping in to say hello. I had met Philip when we were at staff college together. Ian hosted Sir John and his wife for the night – I was off on a team supper with the SAR crews so wasn't with them for dinner. The next morning, breakfast was very different from the day before. It was in the dining room; there was a steward; and there were kippers. Great fun, and it isn't often a minister asks you over breakfast what one thing about the RAF medical services you wanted him to take back to MOD for investigation. It was the most useful kipper I've ever eaten.

I had another, less grand, visit to Leuchars to visit their mountain rescue team. They had identified what they thought was a useful bit of kit for immobilising casualties while transporting them, recommended to them by a civilian doctor in Dundee who worked with another mountain rescue team. Would I have a look and give my opinion? I flew up to Edinburgh from Heathrow first thing in the morning, taking with me a large briefcase into which I had stuffed my flying suit. This was 1987, so when at check-in they noticed I had a knife in my bag – the survival knife fitted to my flying suit– all that happened was that a very apologetic security man explained that he would have to give it to the cabin crew, who would let me have it back as I got off the aircraft. How times change.

When I got to Leuchars I discovered that the civilian doctor was Melvyn Thompson, who had been in my year at medical school (and whose opinion was therefore almost by definition reliable), and that the kit was indeed excellent. I would recommend its adoption. Job done. Then I noticed the mountain rescue team grinning among themselves. Would I be prepared to put my money where my mouth was, and be abseiled down a cliff strapped to the kit? If you want to retain any credibility there's really only one answer to that. It was an interesting experience, but I'm still here.

As part of their routine inspection, I would visit each of the flying stations once a year to review and advise on the practice of aviation medicine. I tended to group them geographically to minimise the travel hassle ("the East Anglia Visit"; "the Scottish Visit" etc.). Most of the time I drove myself in an RAF staff car. This was always tedious because, at that time, RAF vehicles did not have radios. There were some particularly prolonged journeys. The first time I went to RAF Brawdy, near Haverfordwest in West Wales, I couldn't believe quite how far Wales went on after Cardiff and Swansea.

I had of course been on the receiving end of such visits earlier in my career and so understood the game. The last thing any SMO wants is some interfering staff officer from headquarters poking his nose into things and looking for problems. Diversionary tactics are necessary. As much of the time as possible should be spent visiting the flying squadrons and talking to the aircrew (who will have been encouraged – I hesitate to say bribed– to tell me how wonderful the SMO is), and of course to get him airborne in whatever aircraft they have. Undoubtedly Bullsh*t Baffles Brains; and of course I did stick my nose where they would rather I didn't. However I'm glad to say that there was usually a clear correlation between a visit where your feet hardly touched the ground (literally) and a well-run aviation medicine practice.

Perhaps the best exemplar of this was a visit to RAF Northolt. I was asked to arrive early in order to join an HS125 flight delivering VIPs round the South of England so that I would understand the stress under which the aircrew worked. I had no sooner landed from that when I was put into a Gazelle helicopter and flown down the Thames through London. I was particularly pleased that, as we flew past the Houses of Parliament, we experienced the turbulence that everyone does at that point and which is always attributed to an excess of hot air. By the time I got back to Northolt and had called on the station commander, it was time for lunch. To make the point, I insisted on going to the medical centre and looking at some documentation; but of course everything I was shown in the time available was in perfect order. Unfortunately that particularly effective SMO left the service shortly afterwards to take up a very lucrative civilian job.

One morning at his staff meeting, Eddie Simpson read to us a letter from Air Commodore Jim Hall, then the Director of Health and Research for the RAF. He was taking his turn as chairman of the preventive medicine group of the Commonwealth Defence Science Organisation, and was to chair their biennial meeting which was to be held in Kuala Lumpur. He was putting out a request for papers to be considered for the meeting. I made a slightly snide remark to the effect that there was no point, for there certainly wouldn't be any travel funds to take someone from the RAF out to the meeting. Eddie responded rather sharply that if anyone *did* have a paper accepted, then he would make sure that funds would be available. The game was on.

I had been reflecting with some colleagues about medical standards for flying and the need to have enough pilots. If you select only those whose vision (say) is exceptional, then you will have a wonderfully fit group of pilots; but possibly not enough to fill all the cockpits. On the other hand, if you lower the standards too much, your cockpits will be full but their occupants won't be very effective. I produced a philosophical paper entitled 'Medical Standards – How Exclusive Should We Be?' To my immense delight it was accepted, and Eddie was true to his word and found the funds to allow me to go. Even better was that Jim Hall felt the paper didn't fit neatly into any of his subgroups, so he made it the keynote paper for the conference.

Leaving the UK for Malaysia in January is always a good move. Even better was that the RAF travel experts had decided that it was cheapest for me to travel via Hong Kong taking the regular trooping flight, wait there for three days, fly to Kuala Lumpur for the conference then return to Hong Kong at the end for another three days; and finally fly home on the trooper. I wasn't about to complain. On the way out I was put up at the Army Hospital mess in Kowloon, and arranged to visit RAF Sek Kong where I was delighted that Ah May, the tea lady in the medical centre, still remembered me. On the way back I was "on board HMS Tamar" – that is, in the Royal Navy wardroom on Hong Kong Island, and was able to revisit many old haunts.

The conference itself was enormous fun, although I would be the first to admit that it didn't push back the frontiers of science very much. A lot of different nations were represented, and many wore their national dress for the formal events in the evenings. To see a Surgeon Captain of the Nigerian Navy in his traditional colourful dress is a rare sight. It soon became apparent that the ministers of Health and Defence in Malaysia, who were co-hosting the conference, were in some sort of struggle for influence, and each sought to outdo the other with their hospitality. I was not aware of any of the delegates complaining about that. After a couple of evenings of being far too hot in suit and tie while the locals wore their much more appropriate batik dress, most of the "old commonwealth" contingent (UK, Canada, New Zealand and Australia) had an outing to a local tailor's to get ourselves kitted out with batik as well. It was much more comfortable, and our hosts took it as a compliment.

The world of military aviation medicine is a fairly small one and the three services tended to help each other out as required. A particular treat was the Army Air Corps' air show at Middle Wallop in Hampshire. They put on an excellent display of all sorts of army flying, but the need to provide medical cover for all possible eventualities led them to ask for help from the RAF and the RN. It was a great get-together, and fortunately we never had to put into action any of the disaster plans for which we had prepared and practised. The highlight of the show was what everyone called the "mass airmiss", where about forty helicopters flew in line abreast over the airfield. It was a wonderful sight, but we were all quite pleased when it was over safely.

The RAF had a bombing range at a place called Donna Nook, on the Lincolnshire coast. As I was sitting quietly in my office one morning I had a phone call from the range officer there to tell me that they had found the forearm of a WWII airman on the high water mark; what were they to do about it? I wasn't sure that dealing with the limbs of long-dead airmen was necessarily my responsibility, but

I didn't feel I could just dismiss it. I asked how he knew that it was the arm of a WWII airman. The flesh had rotted, he said, leaving the bones of a hand clearly palpable under the remains of a fur glove which is what bomber aircrew wore at that time.

Bomber Command lost over 55,000 aircrew in WWII. The vast majority of them had set off from Lincolnshire. It was all very plausible, and the last thing anyone would want to do would be to dishonour a colleague who had made the ultimate sacrifice. After a little thought I realised, with a certain amount of relief, that the first people to be involved needed to be the police and the coroner. I suggested that the range officer should contact his local police in the first instance.

A couple of hours later he called back, a little embarrassed. There is a colony of seals at Donna Nook. What had been washed up was in fact the flipper of a seal, long dead and detached from its body. A seal's skeleton has bones, similar to those in a human hand, in its flipper, and of course, by definition, it has a sealskin glove. So "The Phantom Hand of Donna Nook" was no more than a flipper from an unfortunate seal. Relief all round.

Although manning was no longer my personal problem, we were all aware that it was a struggle to keep all our posts filled. At one point the SMO at RAF Akrotiri, in Cyprus, was taken ill and admitted to hospital. We had used up any spare capacity we had, and no one had anyone to lend us. The two junior MOs at Akrotiri were just about coping, but they needed some top cover as well as another MO. We discussed the problem at the staff meeting. I was about to go off to RAF Goose Bay, in Canada, to look into a minor problem with MOs accompanying the squadrons who went out there for advanced training. But I was also still, at least on paper, appointable to a GP job. I was the solution. My visit to Goose Bay was postponed, and off I went to Cyprus.

I had never been to Cyprus, and was keen to see it, not least because I had my eyes on a future posting to command the RAF Hospital there. I threw myself into the job with great gusto, assuring the two juniors that I would do four nights' cover out of the seven I would be on the island. I had forgotten how hard out-of-hours on call can be overseas. On my second night the station commander, Group Captain Colin Adams, who had been a flying instructor on my University Air Squadron (and from whom I had bought the red MGB which was my transport when I was a medical cadet), invited me over for drinks. Halfway through my first tomato juice I was called out and didn't finish seeing patients until 11 pm, when I went to bed exhausted only to be wakened again at 3am. The very first patient in the very first surgery I took was a lady who wanted an intrauterine contraceptive device fitted. I hadn't done that for some years, but fortunately female anatomy hadn't changed much in the interval. And so it went on. I was looking forward to a good rest on the flight home, but even that hope was dashed when I was detailed to be the escort for an (admittedly not too demanding) aeromedical evacuation back to UK. When I got back, my office felt like a haven of relaxation by comparison.

Shortly after that I did have my trip to Goose Bay. I flew out in a VC10 which was doing a sort of wandering journey delivering people to and about North America. Goose Bay is a seriously isolated place. At the time there were only a few roads joining the various settlements in the area, but no road connection to the rest of Canada, and the only way in or out was by air or sea. Its climate was pretty fierce too. All the buildings were joined by underground tunnels so that you didn't need to go outside to get about the base in the bitterly cold winter. All the parking places were fitted with electrical sockets so that, when you parked your car you could plug in the heater which all the cars had fitted under the bonnet, to prevent a complete freeze-up. Fortunately I was there in the summer.

I had my meeting with the RAF Officer Commanding. I was shown round the base and its medical facilities, and discussed our mutual problem of how the medical officers travelling with the flying squadrons interacted with the local base facilities. We had a civilised but full and frank discussion, and fairly soon resolved the situation to our mutual satisfaction. It was another day until I could hitch a lift on the next flight back to UK, so I sought out the Canadian Forces SAR helicopter flight at Goose. I discovered that one of the pilots on the flight had done an exchange tour with the RAF, and had worked at RAF Leconfield with a friend of mine called Tony Eley. Tony and I had been junior medical officers at Bruggen together. He left the RAF at the end of his short service commission to be a GP in Derby, but when the Royal Auxiliary Air Force (RAuxAF) set up a reserve aeromedical evacuation squadron, Tony joined it. He was the CO of the squadron when it was deployed to take part in the 1991 Gulf War – the first RAuxAF unit to be deployed to war since WWII. His unit performed well, and he got a very well earned OBE in the campaign honours.

As I had hoped, the Canadians offered to take me on a training trip to watch their procedures and see something of the country. There were thousands of acres of bleak marsh, moor and lakes. There were also herds of moose. Flying alongside a lake, we saw one herd of moose completely immersed, with only their nostrils above water. "That'll be the blackflies," said the pilot. "They drive you wild and the moose sometimes run into the water to avoid them." I was slightly sceptical that flies could be that bad, so the crew put me on the ground and promised to return within five minutes. As soon as the helicopter's downdraught had gone, the flies started. I struck out at them, ran, dodged and did everything else I could, but they had me almost completely covered within a couple of minutes. I was very glad indeed when the returning helicopter first blew them away then picked me up and carried me to safety. Having holidayed on the west coast of Scotland during my youth, I thought I knew about midges. Labrador blackflies are in a different league.

Air Vice-Marshal John Thompson, Goose Bay's Air Officer Commanding (AOC), had been visiting during my spare day, and the next day was going to pilot the C130 Hercules on which I was to return to the UK. It isn't every day you have an AOC as your pilot.

The aircraft was carrying a load of mixed freight, and the AOC's Aide-de-Camp and myself were the only people on board apart from the crew. Hercules passenger facilities are basic. During the take-off and climb we sat on canvas seats at the side of the fuselage, strapped in for safety. However, after that, when we could take our seat belts off, we climbed up on to the cargo nets which help to restrain the load. When you find a suitable gap between two pallets, the net makes a very comfortable hammock. I slept peacefully while the AOC flew me home.

We had a United States Air Force (USAF) Flight Surgeon in the PMO's department at Strike Command. He was part of the RAF/USAF exchange programme. As the other half of the exchange we had an RAF medical officer based at the USAF School of Aerospace Medicine at Brooks Air Force Base in San Antonio, Texas. When I arrived at Strike the incumbent was Colonel Drew Brueder, who had a wife and twelve children. He was succeeded by Colonel Louis Royal, who was unmarried and had no children. Louis was a very happy-go-lucky sort of guy. Together with his friend Doug Douville, he had chosen to study for the Master's in Public Health, which is part of the USAF aerospace medicine training, at Tulane University in New Orleans. They chose Tulane not for the academic value it would offer, but because of the entertainment and other benefits that spending a year in New Orleans would produce. They had had a great time, and Louis would often regale me with stories about their adventures while they were on the course. I began to feel that I knew quite a lot about Doug Douville. This turned out to be useful, because in mid 1988 I was told that I was to be posted to the other RAF/USAF medical exchange post, at Andrews Air Force Base (AFB) in Washington DC, where Doug was the Chief of Aerospace Medicine.

10

Across the Pond

Our journey to America was interesting to say the least. Not long before we were due to fly out, Vivien managed to trip over the dog and hurt her ankle. I examined it but, as she could still walk satisfactorily, announced confidently that she hadn't broken it. A couple of days later, with her still hobbling, we took the children to a concert in the Barbican. With seats up at the back of the circle, Vivien struggled to climb the steps and declared that she was going to see a *proper* doctor next day. Our GP fully supported my diagnosis but, to keep his patient happy, sent her for an X-ray. This showed what Vivien had suspected all along: her ankle was indeed broken. It needed to be plated and screwed. The timing could not have been much worse but, fortunately, the RAF Hospital at Halton was able to operate almost immediately. Our move to Washington was complicated by the fact that Vivien was still on crutches but she flew out as a "reverse" aeromedical evacuation – with me as the escort. Given that I was the one who had missed the fracture in the first place, she might have preferred someone else.

We were met at the airport by my predecessor, Wing Commander Martyn Read. He took us to our hotel, and handed us a list of "realtors" – estate agents. That was when we first realised we were going to have to learn a new language. After our initial briefing at the embassy the next day, our first task was to find somewhere to live. We also needed to get cars – you can't function in DC without wheels. We had a rather tense few days, not helped by jet lag, before we finally found a house the right size, within our budget and convenient for both Andrews AFB and the Embassy. It was just out of DC, across the Potomac in Northern Virginia (a phrase real Virginians regarded as an oxymoron), in a district of Springfield called Saratoga. We had been told that it was usual to rent our furniture. We were slightly anxious about the idea, envisaging some rather tired, thrift shop type stuff, but when Vivien was whisked off to a smart furniture warehouse our anxieties disappeared. They had room after furnished room for her inspection, all laid out like a show house, and it was very much a case of "one of those, two of those, and some more like that, please". We bought a couple of second-hand cars – fortunately, Vivien was able to drive an automatic. Then it was down to work.

Until the early 1980s there had been an aviation medicine staff officer on the defence staff in the British Embassy in Washington DC. The post had been cut in the course of cost-saving measures, but since both the RAF and the USAF valued the existence of a British liaison officer in that specialty, they had set up exchange posts. The RAF had a Flight Medical Officer in the headquarters of USAF Systems Command, their research and development organisation whose headquarters were at Andrews AFB in Washington DC, and the USAF had a Medical Officer Pilot – a Pilot Physician, as the Americans call it – based at the RAF IAM at Farnborough, where he would have access to a great deal of experimental flying. Both sides were happy, and the Americans were content that the Brit at Systems Command would spend a significant amount of time at the Embassy furthering liaison work which would benefit everyone. Martyn introduced me to the people I needed to know at the Embassy and at Systems Command, including Lieutenant Colonel Doug Douville about whom I had heard much from Louis Royal, and with whom I would be working closely.

At the end of the week Martyn flew back to the UK. We took him and his wife Di to the airport to see them off. After that, we picked up our spaniel, Toby, who had flown out the same day. He had travelled in a specially built "flight kennel" and, being a well-brought-up dog, was determined not to soil it in the nine hours or so he spent on the aeroplane. We picked him up from the collection point in a warehouse. The customs officer, passing him over, said, "Welcome to the colonies, dog." You wouldn't get that at an American airport these days. Toby immediately broke away, jumped out of the loading bay, and stood in the grass doing the longest wee I have ever seen a dog do in my life. It seemed to go on for five minutes. He clearly hadn't slept much, presumably because he didn't understand what was happening (have you ever tried to explain to a spaniel that he's going to fly the Atlantic in a box in the hold of an aircraft, and that his Master will meet him at the other end?), and once he had wagged his tail at us, collapsed in the car and slept all the way to his new home.

While we were moving in at Saratoga, some of our neighbours had come out to say hello and welcome us. We became particularly friendly with the couple who lived opposite, Bob and Beverley Goodwin, and their children Marta and Tate. Bob was a Colonel in the US Army, working at one of the many military bases in the Washington area. We had told them that we too had two children, but that they were at boarding school back in the UK. The day after Toby arrived, I was giving him his first long walk for a couple of weeks. On the way back I met Beverley, and explained that Toby had just flown over. Beverley looked puzzled. "Have I got this right," she said, "you've left your children behind but brought your dog?" Put like that, it did seem a little odd.

Systems Command was one of a number of organisations at Andrews AFB. It controlled much of the USAF research and development work. From my point of view, two of the most interesting units were the USAF School of Aerospace Medicine (SAM), at Brooks AFB in San Antonio, Texas, and the Aerospace

Medicine Research Laboratory (AMRL), at Wright Patterson AFB in Dayton, Ohio. I was able to visit AMRL shortly after my arrival, and see something of the work they were doing on the development of flying equipment and life support systems for aircrew.

Not long after I got to Systems Command I was given a clinical problem to investigate. The prototype B2 "stealth" bomber was being built under strict secrecy by a small number of people in what was always referred to as "a classified location". The B2 was constructed of new materials, some of which in theory might be harmful to human health during the construction process. Because of this, the workers received regular medical screening and review. After one such screening, about three-quarters of the workers were found to have abnormal liver function tests. There was inevitable anxiety that this might be an adverse effect of the construction materials. I was given a heap of documentation, all their medical records and details of all the chemicals being used, and asked to give my opinion. As I got stuck into it I realised that this was probably as much a test for me to check on my competence. After a lot of reading, digging into reference books and seeking even more information, I was able to show that the liver function test abnormalities all resulted from different causes (alcohol, old malaria, excess use of over-the-counter medication, etc.) and that none could be attributed to the materials used in manufacture – an opinion backed up to some extent by the fact that a quarter of those exposed to the same materials had no abnormalities at all. My report was accepted and passed up the line. I always felt a particular affection for the B2 after that, and was delighted to be one of the first to see it in the flesh when it was flown over to Andrews for Systems Command personnel to see the results of their labours.

We had flown out to Washington in October. Just before Christmas, we were at the annual Drinks and Christmas Carols party in the embassy. Halfway through it Sir Anthony Acland, the ambassador, interrupted the singing to say that he had just been told of a crash involving an aircraft flying from London to the USA. This was Pan Am flight 103, brought down over Lockerbie in Scotland by a bomb. An RAF colleague nearby went white. Group Captain David Angela knew that his son was coming out to the USA sometime that evening, but as young people tend to do, his son hadn't let his parents know which flight or when to expect him. They had a dreadful hour or so before they could confirm that he had not been killed with the 259 others on Pan Am 103.

As part of my introduction and orientation to the USAF, I attended the two-week Global Medicine course and the one-week Operational Aeromedical Problems course at SAM a couple of months after I arrived. There was a week between the two courses, and the embassy arranged that during that time I would visit the joint RAF/USAF pilot training programme at Sheppard Air Force Base in Wichita Falls, in the north of Texas.

San Antonio is famous, not just among Texans, as the home of The Alamo. Here Davy Crockett, he of the hat, and Jim Bowie, he of the eponymous knife, were among a small group of frontiersmen who held out in the old mission station against overwhelming odds during the struggle for Texan independence from Mexico. They were eventually defeated but their exploits have never been forgotten and "Remember the Alamo" is a battle cry of the American military to this day. San Antonio itself is a beautiful city: despite its large military presence it has a relaxed, laid-back atmosphere due to its comfortable climate and its heritage of Spanish and American culture and architecture. During our time across the pond, it became one of our favourite American cities. Its inhabitants are civilised and friendly, as are many Texans, despite their reputation among the other forty-nine states for being obnoxious, braggart and materialistic. Texas is sufficiently confident not to have to take itself too seriously; for example, their slogan "Don't mess with Texas" was actually part of an anti-litter campaign.

Over the weekend in the middle of the Global Medicine course I headed south, to visit the Confederate Air Force (CAF) at

Harlingen, Texas and Mexico. I had been reassured that the CAF was not a racist lynch mob, but rather a slightly eccentric club of people who restored and flew vintage aircraft. And so it was. All members were Colonels. Their commander was the entirely fictitious Colonel Jethro Culpepper; by their clubhouse ("The CAF Officers' Club") was a patch of mint marked "Solely for the use of Colonel Jethro Culpepper in the preparation of his Mint Juleps". The members were most welcoming and I spent a happy morning wandering round their flight line talking to them, admiring their handiwork and watching various old machines flying.

I then drove further south to Brownsville, Texas, on the Mexican Border. As someone who grew up in the heyday of the Western, crossing the Rio Grande into Mexico was going to be a memorable moment. It wasn't. At that point the Rio Grande was a mere trickle, getting into Mexico was free of formalities and that part of it didn't have a lot worth seeing. I wandered round for an hour or so, then headed back to the USA. At the border post I produced my passport and identity card. Because I was in the USA on NATO business, I didn't have a visa, but rather used a document called a NATO travel order, which, together with my RAF identity card, allowed me multiple entries into the USA. The border guard, a notable exception to my generalisation that Texans are civilised and friendly, glanced at my documents and said, "In there." I found myself in a grotty room with three scruffy-looking Latinos whom I assumed were Mexican. This did not look good, but after a few minutes I was summoned out to see the border guard again. "What is this thing?" he said, pointing at the NATO travel order. I explained. "You cain't come in here with that," he said.

Of course, I could, but I was worried that if I got too abrupt with him he was probably going to lock me up for twenty-four hours while he checked it out. "Our countries are both members of NATO, you know," I volunteered (he scowled at me), "and as well as getting back to your wonderful country I especially want to get back to my car, which is on a parking meter and about to run out of time." The banality of that seemed to swing it for him. "Through you go," he said, "and don't come back to Brownsville any time soon." I wasn't about to.

Back at Brooks I was made very welcome by Squadron Leader Richard Harding and his wife Letitia. Richard was the other RAF medical exchange officer, who had come to SAM from IAM for three years. There were a number of other British military officers in the San Antonio area, and they met up from time to time. It being the 25th of January, they were having a Burns Night celebration – they had even got hold of some haggis. Richard and Letitia invited me to go along with them. Dress for the evening was "Texan", so I went to a Western Store and bought myself a Stetson and some cowboy boots. It was an unusual outfit to wear for dancing the Gay Gordons.

During my time in San Antonio I lived in a suite in the Visiting Officers' Quarters at Brooks AFB. Before my visit to Sheppard AFB Vivien was to join me there. When I went to meet her at the airport I wore my new Stetson and boots, leaning against the wall the way they do in Westerns. She almost walked past me. Back at Brooks we went to the BX (Base Exchange – the base supermarket) to get some food. We were chatting as we moved up the checkout line. When we got to the checkout the saleslady said in a broad Texan drawl, "Y'all ain't from round here, are ya?" We agreed. "Y'all from Louisiana?" We tried to explain, but I'm not sure she got it. It was a bit like the day I had told someone I came from Scotland, only to be asked, "Would that be Scotland, Pennsylvania?"

The day Vivien arrived it was warm and sunny – we had strolled in shirtsleeves along San Antonio's Riverwalk, a former broken-down part of town now restored into a recreational area full of restaurants. As we set out next day for Wichita Falls, it began to get colder – much colder. By the time we were halfway there it was snowing, and soon the snow was freezing on the outside of the car – even on the bonnet despite the hot engine inside. We got there OK, but found that we were holding our breath when moving between our car and our accommodation because breathing the very cold air hurt.

The RAF contingent gave us a warm welcome, and that evening took us to a performance of the musical *Cats*. The next day I met and chatted to the RAF personnel and looked round the training set-up, while Vivien was entertained by a local American couple who volunteer to meet new overseas arrivals to Sheppard and introduce them to the local area, including pointing out the best shops – Vivien took full advantage of that.

Our drive back to San Antonio was much less eventful, although when we pulled off the Interstate into a dusty little hamlet to find something to eat, we were objects of considerable interest as the only "strangers in town" for some time. Vivien and her shopping went back to Washington and I went on to the next course.

About this time we realised that we really were beginning to talk American. Some of it comes quickly and you can't avoid it; you have to say gasoline or you won't get your car filled up. Other words sneak in. Talking with the military, you can only say "missile" for so long. Quite soon it becomes "miss'l". In my case, total immersion at Systems Command undoubtedly accelerated the process. America has a reputation for never using one word when three words will do. My all-time favourite was a building at Andrews AFB called the "Morale, Welfare and Recreation Logistics Support Facility". In the RAF we called it the Sports Store.

In the same way that I had visited the various stations in Strike Command, so at Systems Command we carried out what were known as "Staff Assistance Visits" to bases in the Command. This was a euphemism; they were inspections just the same. Those we visited referred to us as "seagulls" – they fly in, eat your sandwiches, crap all over you and fly away again. I particularly enjoyed the visit we made to Edwards AFB in California. The Chief of Aerospace Medicine there, Lieutenant Colonel "Peach" Taylor, went on to become a Lieutenant General and Surgeon General of the USAF. The hospital commander, Lieutenant Colonel Geoff McCarthy, was about to go to the UK as the other end of my exchange, so it was good to have a chance to meet him. Geoff had been drafted into the USAF and trained as a pilot, after which he had served with the US forces in Europe. When he left at the end of his engagement he had trained as a doctor, then rejoined the USAF in the medical corps. As a physician pilot he was looking forward to the experimental flying he would get at IAM. During the time he was in the UK, the cold war came to an end and travel to Eastern Europe became possible. Geoff had the slightly surreal experience of visiting a military airfield in East Germany which had been his target when he had served as a pilot. He admitted this to the people he spoke to on the base, and was made especially welcome; perhaps because he hadn't actually bombed them after all.

I had never flown beyond Mach 1 (through the sound barrier). Given that it was first done by Chuck Yeager at Edwards AFB, I was very pleased when Geoff offered to take me flying in a T-38 to do a "boom run". As I had been warned, in an aircraft designed to do so it is all something of an anticlimax. I accelerated in a shallow dive and watched the speed build up. The Mach-meter hovered a bit just below Mach 1, then suddenly went over it. There's only the slightest vibration, and of course the noise is far behind you. I was aware, however, that our fuel consumption had gone up significantly. It was a lovely sunny day, and the Mojave desert is a great place to fly over. Another flying ambition achieved.

My liaison job at the embassy brought me all sorts of requests. There was a steady stream of people trying to interest me in their amazingly wonderful bits of aeromedical and flying equipment, most of which could be dismissed almost immediately as verging on the lunatic; but you got the occasional idea worth following up. One day I was approached by a USAF research organisation asking if I could obtain details of damage and injuries caused by German bombs in the London Blitz of 1940. I pursued the subject through the usual sources, and found that we did indeed have such records – a large amount and in astonishing detail. There were records of exact damage to individual buildings and precise numbers and types of injury. How anyone had time to do this as we fought for our very existence I don't know, but it was exactly what the Americans were looking for. When I asked them what they wanted it for they were rather guarded at first, but when they had finished they gave me a full briefing. They had developed a computer program to estimate likely casualties in the event of an air attack on an airfield in Europe. You entered a digital map of "your" airfield, put together an attack package such as you might expect from the likely enemy and pressed the button. The program told you how many casualties of which type you could expect in each building on the airfield. The research was being done by personnel staff, to plan for replacements and reinforcements, but it was obviously enormously useful for medical planning as well. I hurried to the embassy to report it back to the MOD for further action. I felt very pleased with myself, assessing that the value of this one bit of information had probably paid for the whole of my time in America. Then about three weeks later the Berlin Wall came down and the cold war started coming to an end. The program probably wasn't much use after that.

The government of Belize had asked the UK government for advice on dealing with mass casualties in the event of an aircraft crash at their international airport. The request went up, down and across assorted channels until eventually, probably because I was relatively near, I was sent to carry out the task. The contrast between a huge state like the USA and a small one like Belize was marked. I was met off the aircraft by the Assistant British High Commissioner. My meetings were held in the prime minister's waiting room. However, we worked well together and I was able to help them devise a plan which I am glad to say has yet to be needed. I managed to fit in a visit to some of the beautiful cays – the reef offshore is second in size only to Australia's Great Barrier Reef – and to the Mayan temple at Altun Ha. I stayed with the Air Commander, one of whose "duties" was to put up middle-ranking officers passing through. I was able partly to repay his hospitality by babysitting for him and his wife one evening; I was especially pleased to introduce their two-year-old son to *Bagpuss* via a video I had found. There was something very surreal about watching *Bagpuss* in Belize.

Being a liaison officer meant attending a lot of meetings and conferences – or conventions, as the Americans call them. These were always held in large hotels in large cities around the USA, and always started on a Monday morning. Because of some obscure rule in American civil aviation, if you stayed over Saturday night on a round trip, the airfare was significantly lower than otherwise. As a result I would always travel a day early, which gave me a day to explore the city and its surroundings. Because they were saving so much in airfares, the embassy bean counters were very happy to stump up an extra day's subsistence. Usually Vivien would come with me – although of course I paid for her travel.

The very first meeting I went to was the SAFE association meeting in Las Vegas. The primary objective of the SAFE Association is to stimulate research and development in the fields of safety and survival. All sorts of flying safety equipment was on show and was being extolled by its manufacturers. I was there with my embassy hat on, while Doug Douville represented Systems Command. On the Sunday morning Vivien and I and Doug and his wife Pattie decided to go for champagne brunch in Caesar's Palace. As we approached, I could see a couple of centurions on guard at the entrance. "Ave," I said, rather pompously. "How ya doin' there," they replied. I gave up after that.

The meeting was held in a large hotel, and to get from the hotel part to the conference suite you had, of course, to go through the casino. I was not prepared to demean the Queen's uniform by wearing it in such a seedy place, so I took the long way round outside the building. I was not surprised to come across other Brits doing the same.

The Association of Military Surgeons of the United States (AMSUS) held an annual meeting devoted to advances in military medicine which was attended not only by the Americans but by a large number of invited international guests who were treated right royally. The Director General of RAF Medical Services ("the DG") was always invited. During my time in the USA the DG was Air Marshal Sir Nigel Mills, who was also Surgeon-General of the British Armed Forces. Although he brought his staff officer with him, inevitably I was involved on my side of the pond in making sure that all his arrangements ran smoothly. The meeting was a bit of a three-ring circus, with presentations going on in several different rooms at the same time, and Sir Nigel and I would divide up the programme, each going to separate presentations and comparing notes afterwards. Although the meeting was thoroughly enjoyable, and the hospitality outstanding (they even gave us a medal for attending), getting the most out of it was quite hard work.

One AMSUS meeting was held at the Opryland Hotel in Nashville, Tennessee, home of country and western music and the Grand Old Opry. We got tickets for the Grand Old Opry one night, and during the evening it came out – mostly from Pamela, Sir Nigel's wife – that he had a certain penchant for Dolly Parton and that the next day was his birthday. We arranged for a birthday card, purportedly from Ms Parton, to be delivered to his room the following morning. He was very pleased.

The biggest of the three annual meetings on my calendar was that of the Aerospace Medical Association (AsMA). There was always a very large UK contingent, with many of the team from IAM, and of course the DG. In the middle of the conference week, the DG would give a drinks party for all our international friends and allies. There was never much funding for this, so the standard procedure was for the DG and his staff officer to have adjoining rooms; the communicating door would be opened for the party, with all the furniture being moved into one room in which was also the bar, while the other served as the reception room. The bath in the "bar" room became a gigantic ice bucket. It always went down well, and was seen as one of the highlights of the meeting. There was a very amusing moment at the beginning of one AsMA meeting when the DG discovered that, while he and his (male) staff officer had rooms next to each other, they did not interconnect. They went down to reception to change that. At that time homosexuality was illegal in both British and American armed forces, and the looks they got as the reception staff jumped to the wrong conclusion were wonderful to behold.

Each year, before or after the AsMA meeting, the DG would spend a week visiting various aerospace medicine facilities in the USA. It was my job to organise and arrange the visit. It was always slightly fraught, because getting things wrong could quickly ruin your career prospects. On the other hand, if it worked, you had made your mark with the boss. I never had any disasters but there were a few exciting moments.

One year the tour started at SAM, where they laid on a breakfast briefing at 0730. Sir Nigel's staff officer, Squadron Leader Phil Bush, and I had flown down to San Antonio the day before. Sir Nigel couldn't get away that early, so flew in to San Antonio direct from London. He was exhausted anyway, and his flight was delayed. He didn't get in until almost midnight. Next morning we fronted up for the briefing, had a tour of the laboratories at SAM, then flew to Eglin AFB in Florida for the next part of the visit. We got there at midday and the USAF gave us lunch in their officers' club, by the beach overlooking the Gulf of Mexico. We had about half an hour to relax after lunch before the official visit started. As he sat in the sun looking at the white sand and appreciating the lapping of the waves and the gentle warm breeze, Sir Nigel suggested that if we wanted to have a mutiny and stay there for the rest of the day, he would be happy to lead it. Nobly, we went on.

Visiting the School of Army Aerospace Medicine at Fort Rucker, Alabama, we sensibly got there the night before. When I was getting dressed the next morning I heard a military band playing outside somewhere near my room. I couldn't see it out of my window so I stood on the luggage stand. It wasn't meant for standing on, collapsed, and propelled my eye towards a door handle. It really hurt, and I thought I had lost an eye. I was very relieved when I got to a mirror and saw that it was still there. I made no mention of it, but as the morning progressed, so did the swelling in my eye. Eventually, the Commandant at Fort Rucker, who was giving an opening presentation, stopped, looked at my eye, which by this time had almost completely closed, and insisted on it being checked by an ophthalmologist. All was well, but I spent the rest of the visit with a dramatic black eye.

Driving between two visits somewhere on US Interstate Highway 10, the southernmost cross-country highway, we needed to travel east to our next destination. I joined the Interstate via what I was certain was the correct on-slip, and we drove on. After about ten minutes, Sir Nigel said, "Iain, are you sure we're going east?" I pride myself on my navigation, so he got as dusty an answer as a Wing Commander can reasonably give to an Air Marshal. "Then why," he said, "is the setting sun in front of us?"

Pause. Tell staff officer in the back to get out the map. Think hard about how we came on. Fortunately realise quite quickly that the road is going round in a large loop to avoid a couple of lakes. Whatever direction we're pointing right now, overall we are going east. Relax. Probably still have a career.

The final part of one tour was a visit to AMRL at Wright Patterson AFB. We were to arrive at midday on a Thursday, have a presentation in the afternoon, and tour the labs the next morning. It was an American public holiday weekend. The Americans were keen to get off early on the Friday, and we were keen to have the Friday afternoon free to visit the Aviation Museum on the base. When we changed aircraft on our way to Ohio – I think it was in Atlanta, it usually was – our connection was delayed and delayed and it became apparent that we weren't going to get to "Wright-Patt" until too late. That would mean that the whole programme would slip by half a day and we wouldn't have time to go to the museum. Well, you can't have everything.

When we eventually did get to Wright-Patt, while the official introductions were taking place I was approached by a USAF colleague whom I knew well from my various dealings with AMRL. They really wanted to get away at lunchtime on Friday. Could I persuade my "general" – they never quite got to grips with RAF ranks – to stick with the programme for tomorrow and have the presentation that evening? I couldn't believe our luck. Sir Nigel needed no persuading, and I got lots of brownie points from the Americans for making their lives that bit easier. And we got to go to the museum.

Our children were at boarding school in Scotland, but flew out each school holiday to join us. With a month each at Christmas and Easter, and two months in the summer, they spent a total of almost a year with us in Washington. They were in their early to mid teens, and well placed to take advantage of what it had to offer. There were of course a number of "embassy brats", so they had a ready-made group of friends and acquaintances. The embassy ran a teenagers' Christmas dance, and on their first visit to us Clare and Robin (the latter in an old DJ of mine pinned and sewn so as to just about fit him) were quite overawed by it all. After that they were less so, and each year we heard less about their team and its exploits. At least we never had to bail them out.

We had some very happy family holidays. We headed off at various times to the north and west, visiting most of the states in the north-west quadrant of the USA. We visited Yellowstone and Yosemite, San Francisco, the Grand Canyon and Death Valley.

One of our best ever holidays we spent on a ranch in Montana. My American friends later had to educate me about the length of the "a's" in both nouns. One evening sitting on the stoop, looking at the biggest moon we had ever seen, Irving, the rancher, told us that he used to play the French horn; and that his old French horn was somewhere in the cellar. Clare told him that she too played the French horn, and that she had her mouthpiece with her (apparently hornblowers do this). Irving found the horn and the two of them gave us an impromptu open-air concert. Another surreal moment – French horns in Montana.

Typically we would hire a people carrier vehicle, which had plenty of room for us to stretch out and for our luggage. Vivien and Clare became ace at negotiating discounts in motels. On one occasion Clare sat clipping out discount coupons from a magazine in the reception area even as Vivien was talking to the receptionist. When we went to a rodeo in a small town outside Denver, Robin decided that he would like a beer. The drinking age in America is twenty-one – a law which is honoured more in the breach than the observance – but as I didn't want to be charged with "contributing to the delinquency of a minor" I wouldn't get him one. He sidled towards the bar to assess his chances. The barmaid spotted him. "D'you want a beer, honey?" Robin was delighted.

The rules about young people driving were different. In Virginia you could get the equivalent of a provisional licence at fifteen years and eight months, and a full licence at sixteen. Both Clare and Robin took maximum advantage of the situation. Clare was able to get a full licence, and to use it together with an International Driving Permit to drive in the UK for a year after our return. When she went to sit her UK driving test, she drove herself to it and, had she failed, would have been able to drive herself home again. Fortunately, she passed. We had come home before Robin could get his full licence, but back at school in Edinburgh he was able to use his provisional licence to convince a bus conductor that he was indeed under sixteen and therefore entitled to a half fare. He got a lot of peer admiration for that.

US employment law didn't allow Vivien to have a full-time job, but she was able to temp. Many wives found that their British accents made them highly sought after as receptionists. Vivien spent a few months working for the wonderfully named National Erectors Association. Having dealt with a caller, she was delighted when he finished by saying "Lady, you're a class act". She also did some supply teaching at the Robert E Lee High School. They don't forget their heroes, those Virginians; but given the current attitude to Confederate memorials, I wonder if it's still called that.

1990 saw the fiftieth anniversary of the Battle of Britain. There was a commemorative service in the National Cathedral in Washington, and because of the anniversary, the RAF's annual Battle of Britain cocktail party, instead of being held in the rotunda – the entertainment venue attached to the main embassy building – took place in the ambassador's residence. We had an RAF band to play for Beating the Retreat, and the salute was taken by Marshal of the Royal Air Force Lord Elworthy. "Sam" Elworthy had been a Battle of Britain pilot and had risen to become Chief of Defence Staff. On his retirement he had returned to his native New Zealand. The Royal New Zealand Air Force was flying him over to London for the celebrations there, with a stopover in Washington to be with us.

In 1990 he was 79. It was a hot, humid September evening in Washington. He was in full dress uniform, and he had just flown in from New Zealand. As he stood on the dais taking the salute I thought he was looking a little grey round the gills (to use a technical medical term). I edged towards the dais to be ready to help him if he were to faint. Which, just after he had taken the salute and the band was marching off, he did. I was able to ease his fall, and a number of others helped me carry him in to a small cool air-conditioned room in the residence. We laid him on a sofa and my "stretcher bearers" went off, leaving me, Lord Elworthy, Sir Anthony Acland and Air Commodore Simon Baldwin, the Air Attaché. After a few minutes sitting in the cooler air and with his jacket unbuttoned, the patient looked rather better. Mr Shand, the ambassador's butler, took an order for drinks. All was going well, so after about ten minutes I thought I would remove myself from the otherwise very senior group. As I rose and indicated that I was about to go, the other three said, virtually in unison, "No, Doctor. Sit down." So I did. After about three-quarters of an hour, Lord Elworthy had made a full recovery and we accompanied him to his car to go back to his hotel.

The cocktail party had ended with Beating the Retreat and all the guests had gone. It had fallen to Vivien to make our farewells to our American guests. Then she had to wait in the ambassador's garden watching his staff lay the table for supper for two on the terrace of the residence while she contemplated that, when I eventually rejoined her, she would have to conjure up supper for two half an hour away in suburban Virginia.

We had heard about Saddam Hussein invading Kuwait while we were on holiday in Montana. Since then the build-up for what was to become the First Gulf War had been going on. At the SAFE meeting that autumn there was a larger than usual number of people from the US Department of Defense and the British MOD with fat cheque books looking for kit they might need in a desert war. One of the units on Andrews AFB was an aeromedical evacuation reception station. In preparation for war it was being expanded greatly so as to cope with a very large number of casualties – indoor tennis courts were being converted into wards. None of the medical officers at Systems Command had a war appointment, so we formed ourselves into an aeromed reception team, and practised with the full-time staff so that we could run a shift for them. Fortunately, in the event there were many fewer casualties than had been anticipated, and the regular full-time staff were able to cope with them all. While we were delighted that there were so few casualties, we were a little disappointed that we hadn't been able to do anything to directly help the war effort.

In May 1991 the Queen paid a state visit to the USA. Towards the end she gave a garden party at the Embassy. All of us on the defence staff were involved in assorted support duties. With our wives, we helped host the many guests. I was part of the Duke of Edinburgh's "snowplough" – the discreet group of a few people who walked in front of the Duke to make sure he had a clear path as he strolled among the guests. At one point Vivien was talking to Jessye Norman, the opera singer. She then realised that on her other side was Jesse Jackson, the civil rights activist. Seizing the opportunity, she introduced one Jess(y)e to another. It soon appeared to Vivien that, while they had never met before, neither was particularly pleased to make the other's acquaintance. She made her excuses and backed away. In the embassy, immediately after the garden party, the Queen received Air Commodore Sir Frank Whittle, the inventor of the jet engine, who now lived in the Washington area. She presented him with the Charles Stark Draper prize awarded by the American National Academy of Engineering for his pioneering work. It was good to see him still being recognised some fifty-five years after his first breakthrough.

By far and away the biggest thing that happened when I was in the USA was that the cold war ended. We watched with disbelief as the Berlin Wall came down, and followed the subsequent break-up of the USSR and problems in the Russian Federation avidly. We had "won" the cold war partly because our science and technology had been much better than the USSR could produce or afford, so Systems Command felt that it had played a very real part, and we were proud of that. Next, of course, came the "Peace Dividend". There were large cuts in armed forces across the world. As part of the cuts, Systems Command was to be disbanded, with its functions being taken over by another Command headquarters based in Ohio.

Ohio is not the best place from which to carry out international liaison. My post basically would not work there. Luckily, I was still playing squash once a week with Colonel Jim Yoder, who had been the chief physician at Systems Command but had moved to be the Chief of Aerospace Medicine at Headquarters USAF at Bolling AFB, also in Greater Washington and only a few miles from Andrews. We discussed the problem over a post-game drink, and came up with the idea of transferring the post to his department. Slightly to our surprise, when we sent the proposal up our chains of command, it was agreed by all within a remarkably short period of time. My last few weeks in the USA were spent organising the move, and the new post was all set up and ready to go when my successor, Group Captain Mike Gibson, arrived.

11

Vale of Health

Winter ended early in Washington in 1991. It was warm by February, and by the time October came and I was about to return to UK I'd had more than enough of the enervating hot, humid climate. I was looking forward to a British autumn. Not long after my return I was turning the corner from Theobald's Road into Gray's Inn Road on the way back to my office in High Holborn in London, when a rain-filled icy blast nearly knocked me over, reminding me that you should be careful what you wish for.

We came back to the UK on the RAF VC10 trooping aircraft from Washington to RAF Brize Norton, and went to spend the weekend in Shropshire with John and Kate Garnons Williams. John had left the RAF and was running his own business, but still flew for one of the RAF Air Experience Flights, which gave Air Cadets the opportunity to go flying in light aircraft. John's flight had Chipmunks, and he had arranged for us to get airborne the next day. I hadn't flown a Chipmunk for nearly twenty years, so I was delighted when it all came back to me and I was able to fly virtually all the sortie myself, including some serious side-slipping to lose height on the final approach, which caused John just a little anxiety.

After a relaxing weekend with the Garnons Williams, we headed for London to start house hunting. As a fairly senior officer – I had been promoted to Group Captain on my return – with twenty-four years' service and returning from an overseas post, I had high priority for allocation of an RAF married quarter. Unfortunately, none was available in the London area. All were occupied, and there was no expectation of a vacancy in the foreseeable future. So we were on our own and it was up to us yet again to find somewhere to rent. That was the downside. The upside was that, provided the house we found was of similar size to the type of married quarter I was entitled to, I would only pay married quarters rent and the MOD would make up the difference.

We stayed in a rather bleak room in the Officers' Mess at RAF Uxbridge, and set out each day for meetings with estate agents – some better than others – until we finally found a house. It was a lovely Victorian end-terrace house in the Vale of Health, in Hampstead. The Vale is a small area totally surrounded by the Heath, with a pond beside it. It was a lovely setting – a classic example of *rus in urbe*. A couple of centuries earlier Constable had painted the pond from the spot where our front door now stood. In the end, we were delighted that there had not been any married quarters available

Once we had found somewhere to live, we went up to our cottage in Scotland for the rest of my disembarkation leave. There we heard the sad news that Sir Nigel Mills had died. He had had cancer for some time, but in the end he went very quickly. He had been a fine leader and I had greatly enjoyed working with him while I was in America.

My new job was as Director of Medical Organisation for the RAF. I was responsible for RAF medical policy, plans and standards, and was Chief of Staff to Air Vice-Marshal Mike Brook, the new DG. I had never worked with him, but our paths had crossed many times over the years. My arrival interview with him confirmed my belief that we could work well together.

The job was going to be particularly demanding because we were negotiating the future size and shape of the RAF medical services following the end of the cold war. I was one officer short on my staff, and despite my pleas to the Director of Medical Personnel – Warwick Pike, now also a Group Captain – no one was available. At one of the DG's staff meetings I was making a great song and dance about it all when the Director of Nursing Services, Group Captain Eithne Hancock, said she thought she might be able to let me have a nursing officer. I didn't especially want a nursing officer. As far as I was aware they had no one who was staff trained and whatever other skills they might have, whoever filled the post was going to have to hit the ground running. Having made such a fuss, however, I didn't really feel I could refuse. So she sent me Squadron Leader Elaine Proud.

Elaine came to us from a very busy tour on the aeromed team. She had been involved with the recoveries of many of the hostages who had been held in the Middle East at that time, a job which was physically and psychologically very demanding. She was a down-to-earth Yorkshirewoman, and it soon became apparent that she was very good at getting to the nub of a problem, would not take waffle or bull from anyone, and was not afraid to say when she didn't know something or was out of her depth, and to ask for help. Despite her lack of formal staff training, she was very good at presenting a summary of a situation either verbally or on paper. She very soon became a valuable part of the team.

One evening, a couple of months after we had settled in to the Vale of Health, we answered the doorbell to find a couple who had just moved in across the road. Their removal van was due to arrive the next day, and they didn't know how it was going to get parked. The road through the Vale was very narrow, and cars were parked everywhere. The answer, we told them, was to knock on people's doors and ask them to move their cars. It was what everyone did – there was no other way. But while they were here, would they like to come in for a drink? They introduced themselves as Leon Morrocco and his wife Jean. They had just returned to the UK after twelve years in Australia, where Leon had been teaching at the College of

Art in Melbourne. Within about twenty minutes we had worked out that we had been at the same New Year's Eve party in Dundee in 1969. Leon's father, Alberto, was head of painting at the College of Art in Dundee, and we had been there with friends whose father knew the Morroccos well.

It was the beginning of what might seem an unlikely friendship – military doctor and artist – which has continued to this day, although saddened by Jean's untimely death in 2016. Over the years we have been to Leon's shows, watched his style develop and followed his career – he is now a Royal Scottish Academician – and we are delighted to have a couple of his paintings on our walls.

At work, my team had got together the overall strategy for the reorganisation of the medical services. The DG had not yet seen it, but I had planned to talk him through it when he returned from a fortnight's leave. Then Air Vice-Marshal John Willis, the Director General of Personnel Services, who was the lead in the Air Member for Personnel's (AMP) department in the restructuring process, dropped over informally one afternoon to talk about our ideas. He liked them, and said he would take a copy of the draft and show it informally to AMP, Air Chief Marshal Sir Sandy Wilson. Next day John Willis phoned back to say that Sandy Wilson also liked it, and would show it informally to the Air Force Board Standing Committee in two days' time. Two days later I got a message back down the line saying they liked the look of the draft, so would I now work to put together the final document.

This was all very well, but these things are supposed to go through careful study and preparation, and it takes weeks to go through the formal process; and now we were in effect committed to an idea which my DG hadn't even heard about, far less studied or agreed. When he returned at the beginning of the next week I went straight in to see him and explain, apologise and grovel. I need not have worried. His ideas about the future were very similar to mine, so I walked away unscathed.

Early in 1992 the Air Attaché in Amman contacted MOD

to say that the Royal Jordanian Air Force (RJAF) was extending an invitation for someone from the RAF to visit and advise on medical provision for the RJAF, with particular reference to aviation medicine. Jordan had supported Iraq in the Gulf crisis of 1990–91, and had lost the backing of some of its aid providers such as ourselves and the USA; there had been a cooling of relations. This invitation was seen as part of a bridge-rebuilding exercise, and would likely have political overtones as well as the medical aspects. After some discussion, the DG decided that I was the appropriate person to send. I agreed.

I went to Jordan in September 1992. The RJAF was as welcoming, helpful and supportive as it could be. After I had met Lieutenant Colonel (Dr) Mohammed Abbadi, the Director of Medical Services of the RJAF, who accompanied me for much of the time, I called on Lieutenant General Ihsan Shurdom, the Chief of Staff. He had been at the RAF staff college with Air Marshals John Thomson and Sandy Wilson and was clearly an Anglophile. He made it clear that he had no false pride and that he wanted a full report with no punches pulled. He assured me of the full cooperation of all his staff, and invited me to call him on "this number" – he scribbled a telephone number on a piece of paper – if I had any problems. Of course, his staff in the office with us all took note of this, and so unsurprisingly, I never had to use it. My next call, on the Surgeon General of Jordan's Royal Medical Service, Major General (Dr) Youssef Goussous, was similarly helpful. I was given an RJAF staff car and driver which remained at my total disposal throughout the visit.

I visited the RJAF main fighter base at Al-Azraq, where as well as looking at the medical centre and their aircrew equipment I flew the Mirage simulator. After this I gave a lecture to the aircrew on "G"-induced loss of consciousness. This hazard was becoming more prevalent at the time, as aircraft manoeuvrability increased causing an inevitable increase in the likelihood that high "G" forces would result in the pilot losing consciousness, often with expensive and fatal results. The question period which followed was gratifyingly robust, reminding me that fighter pilots tend to have the same personality traits whatever nationality they are.

In the middle of my visit, the Base Commander was called away to take an urgent message. He returned grinning from ear to ear. King Hussein had been in America receiving medical treatment, and was to return to his kingdom in three days' time. As he entered Jordanian airspace he would be flying the Royal L1011 Tristar, and the Base Commander had just been instructed to organise and lead a sixteen-aircraft formation to escort the King home.

On our way back to Amman we stopped at Azraq castle, which had been used by King Feisal during the Arab revolt in WWI, and where I was shown the room occupied by Colonel T E Lawrence (Lawrence of Arabia) before he set out on his ill-fated expedition to Deraa. The Jordanians obviously still held "El Orens" in high regard.

The British Air Attaché, Wing Commander Mike Bell, accompanied me on a visit to Petra. As well as exploring the fascinating sandstone ruins, I mounted a camel for the obligatory photograph (Mike stood ready to get one of me falling off; luckily I stayed on). You normally have to pay the camel owner for this, but I didn't. Khalid, my driver, (as Mike translated for me) told the owner that I was a great plenipotentiary from across the sea, that it was an honour for him to have me on his camel, and that he was lucky we weren't charging him for it.

The Jordanians were keen to show me their historic sites, and Mohammed Abbadi took me to Jerash, one of the best-preserved Roman cities in the Near East, and to the castle at Ajlun, originally built in the 12th century by one of Saladin's generals. At both sites we were waved through the entrance gate and allowed to wander freely all over, climbing all about the buildings and exploring like a couple of overgrown schoolboys.

The RJAF Base at Mafraq houses the King Hussein Air Academy, where officer cadets receive military and flying training. Halfway through the tour of their medical centre I realised that it was an almost exact copy of my old medical centre at the RAF College at Cranwell. Not for nothing have we trained many Jordanian officers in Lincolnshire.

One day I accompanied Mike Bell on a visit to Um Qeis, in the north of the country. As we got nearer, the road signs started calling it "Um Qeis (ancient Gadara)". After I'd seen a couple of these signs it dawned on me that this was the site of the incident described in Matthew 8:28–32 where the unfortunate Gadarene swine, having received a devil cast out by Jesus Christ, charged over a cliff to their death. As well as the cliff, we could see the Golan Heights with some of their fortifications, and the Sea of Galilee. It was rather smaller than I had expected. I couldn't envisage it being stormy enough to need divine calming.

I have always been interested in Lawrence of Arabia, and was looking forward to joining a group of Jordanians and expatriate Brits for an evening trip on the Hejaz railway (which Lawrence regularly blew up) into the desert, where there was to be a barbecue and dance. However, King Hussein was going to return to his kingdom that day, and so the trip, along with everything else in Jordan, was cancelled so that the whole country could welcome him back.

Preparations for the King's return began the day before, and numbers of Bedu began to come into Amman from the desert and pitch their tents on vacant lots by roads along the King's planned route from the airport to his palace. I asked at the embassy if I should keep out the way during what was obviously going to be a great outbreak of nationalism, but I was assured not only that I would be safe, but that the locals would be pleased that I had come to watch.

I went on to the roof terrace of my hotel – one of the highest points in Amman – to watch the King's arrival. His Tristar appeared with eight F-5 fighter aircraft in echelon formation off each wing. As he reached the city they all descended and the King "beat up" – there is no other word for it – his capital. At one point all seventeen aircraft flew below me as I stood on the roof. On the television in my room I watched the King's arrival and reception at the airport. He was being driven in a large Mercedes by his brother, Crown Prince Hassan, and his route to the palace was deliberately tortuous so that he could show himself to as many of his people as possible. In front of and behind the Mercedes were members of the "Desert Patrol" – Jordan's equivalent of our Royal Guards – in their smart maroon Land Rovers. Close security was provided by the usual men in suits, dark glasses and what looked like hearing aids, and with bulges under their armpits.

After being driven not very far at all, the King had clearly decided that he couldn't show himself properly to his people from inside the car. So he got out and sat on the roof, with his feet on the bonnet and holding on to the wipers. The close security people didn't look very happy about that. I left my hotel and walked a few hundred yards to a road where the King was due to pass. It was very hot. The whole place was thronging with excited Jordanians determined to show their loyalty to and love for their King. Later, it was estimated that about 1.5 million people, out of a total national population in 1992 of about 4 million, were in Amman that day. Many more tents had been pitched. In front of them sat dignified-looking Bedu in their finest clothes. There were sheep, goats and even a camel tethered alongside to be sacrificed in honour of the King as he drove by. Everyone was ululating loudly, and firearms of various sorts were being discharged into the air. The atmosphere was electric; the scene was mediaeval. It was one of the most extraordinary things I have ever seen.

Once the King had passed and the animals had been sacrificed I went back to my hotel to cool down a bit. Mohammed Abbadi and his team had been on standby throughout the day with their SAR/Casualty Evacuation helicopters ready to deal with casualties. Astonishingly, and despite all the loosing off of firearms, they had no serious problems. Allah is indeed merciful.

My last day was spent finishing off my report and delivering it to the RJAF. Then it was back to London and downsizing. Our plans for reorganisation had been approved, and I was now at the stage of horse-trading exact numbers of posts and personnel with the man from John Willis' department who held the purse strings. I was particularly pleased with a couple of our innovations which had been agreed: the establishment of a Tactical Medical Wing to control the operational parts of the RAF medical services and the setting up of Air Transportable Surgical Support Teams, giving us the ability to provide rapid surgical support to out-of-the-way places with little in the way of sophisticated infrastructure. Over the years both have evolved and developed as part of the first-class casualty recovery and treatment system from which the British Armed Forces now benefit.

Headquarters and their staffs were reduced, and we were closing all but two of our hospitals in the UK, those at Ely in Cambridgeshire and Wroughton in Wiltshire. Wroughton was already our largest hospital, and was to get larger still under the reorganisation plans. The WWII-era wooden huts which housed the outpatients department were to be replaced by a new purpose-built building, the officers' mess was to be enlarged and the RAF Institute of Pathology and Tropical Medicine was to relocate from RAF Halton to RAF Wroughton where a new Institute was to be built. The whole redevelopment would cost over thirty million pounds. I was excited to be posted to Wroughton as the Station Commander, where I would oversee it all.

12

Station Commander

The Queen Mother first came to the Castle of Mey in Caithness in 1952, when I was at primary school in Wick. We were all taken to the airport to welcome her. Her car, of course, flew the Royal Standard. For some time after that, whenever I drew a car, it had a flag on it. I had never really grown out of that idea, and one of the things I was really looking forward to as a station commander was driving around with a flag on my car.

There was more to it than that, of course. Aside from the day-to-day running of the station, there was all the planned building work to be dealt with. Managing my forty-three clinical consultants made herding cats seem like a soft option. All the consultants had direct access to me on "clinical matters". You will not be surprised to learn that their definition of "clinical matters" tended to differ from mine.

RAF Wroughton was on the edge of the Wiltshire Downs. I used to amuse myself by varying my description of exactly where it was. If I said, "It's just south of Swindon," back would come the response "Oh dear." If I said, "It's just north of Marlborough," people would say, "How lovely." Yet it was always in the same place. Although Princess Alexandra's RAF Hospital was by far the largest unit, RAF Wroughton also housed the RAF aeromedical evacuation personnel, who were controlled by Headquarters No 1 Group, and I had a Naval lodger unit – the depot of the Directorate of Naval Recruiting. Wroughton airfield had been a Royal Naval Air Yard where they serviced helicopters. When that closed and the airfield passed to the Science Museum, the Navy left the stores and servicing facilities for their various recruiting activities at RAF Wroughton. The Naval personnel did their share of station duties, and their Officer Commanding took inter-service cooperation to a higher plane by marrying one of my trainee surgeons.

We were close to both RAF Lyneham and RAF Brize Norton, transport bases to which aeromedical evacuation patients would return from overseas, which meant they had a short onward transfer to hospital. "The Troubles" in Northern Ireland were a source of many patients at the beginning of my tour. Later, they came from the former Yugoslavia. During my time at Wroughton, Lyneham was commanded by Group Captain Brian Symes and Brize Norton by Group Captain Alan Kearney, both of whom had been at staff college with me. It made for easy inter-station relations.

Being a station commander was something of a "two for one" job. Although it was never stated explicitly, the station commander's wife was expected to do her bit in running the close-knit small town which was an RAF station, and Vivien found herself chairing the Wives' Club and getting involved in various welfare activities. It was the early days of desktop publishing, and she set up and ran a monthly station newsletter, which was an excellent way of keeping people throughout the station informed about what was going on. Changes in society in general were resulting in this paternalistic approach being questioned more and more, and our particular cohort of station commanders was among the last to follow the traditional pattern.

We moved into the station commander's residence – a large six-bedroomed house based on a Lutyens design which filled that role on many RAF stations. It was designed for entertaining. There was a guest suite where if necessary I would be expected to accommodate any senior visitors, and the ground floor was well laid out for hosting dinners and parties. I was required to do a certain amount of official entertaining, as part of fulfilling the instructions in my Station Commander's Directive to "foster friendly relations with your local civilian community, taking appropriate opportunities to present the Royal Air Force in a good light."

When we entertained formally we (or, to be precise, Vivien) would get help in the shape of a chef and steward from the officers' mess. I did not get involved. When I had dressed and come downstairs I would be banished to the drawing room, where Duncan the steward would bring me a drink. However, on one occasion just before a particularly grand dinner party – the guests included a General and an Air Marshal – I could hear ever-increasing noises coming from the kitchen. I went in to find chef becoming increasingly agitated, as chefs do. The cooker was repeatedly triggering the circuit breaker and his creations were being threatened. The circuit breaker had tripped a couple of times for us over the previous week. I was fairly sure that there were no serious electrical problems, so I got hold of a broom and used the handle to hold the circuit breaker up, keeping my eyes and nose alert for signs of fire. Chef and the steward were horrified. "You can't do that, sir – health and safety." I reminded them that, as the station commander, I could do what I liked; and would they get on with their preparations, please. I stood there holding it until the first guests arrived. The food was perfect and the house didn't burn down. And on the following Monday the electricians checked the circuit and sorted it out.

On another occasion, on a warm summer evening, we were taking pre-dinner drinks out on the terrace. Just then Robin arrived home. He had a holiday job in London and had had a very hot and uncomfortable journey home. The train to Swindon had been packed and had made a number of unscheduled stops. The bus up the hill to Wroughton had broken down and he had had to walk the last mile. He came out on to the terrace to say hello. He knew some of the guests and moved over to talk to them. Without anyone having asked him to, Duncan, the steward, brought Robin a cold beer in a chilled tankard. Robin turned, took it gratefully, said, "Thank you, Duncan," and turned back to the conversation. As he did so I caught his eye. He was at the zenith of his undergraduate left-wing leanings, and was forever having a go at us for our middle-class lifestyle. After our eyes met he never uttered another word on the subject.

The residence came with a housekeeper. We inherited Pat, a solid and reliable lady from Wroughton village, who had been in the job for decades and made it clear to Vivien on day one how the residence was to be run. She was very efficient, and a creature of habit. If it was Wednesday and 10.45am you could be sure she was polishing the brass finger-plate on the door of my dressing room. She told Vivien one day that it was her sixtieth birthday, and that her husband had arranged a "surprise" party for her in the local pub that evening. Next morning she didn't arrive for work. Given what she knew about the party, Vivien wasn't completely surprised. She was horrified, however, when the mess manager arrived with the tragic news of what had happened. Pat and her husband had set out from home to walk to the pub the previous evening. About 100 yards short of the pub Pat dropped down dead. Her husband raced to the pub for help, but as he entered the crowd of friends all started shouting "Surprise!" and singing 'Happy Birthday to You'. It took some minutes to get some sense into the whole awful scene. Although we had other staff to help, the residence was never the same without Pat.

The hospital was in fairly good shape, and those bits that really did need sorting out – like the WWII huts which still housed the outpatients department – were due to be replaced. Just over three years previously we had built a state-of-the-art four-theatre operating suite, and the year before we had got an MRI scanner – the first in the services and the first in our local area. As well as its many clinical uses it served as a revenue generator, for we opened it for use by the local NHS and private hospitals after 1700. Out of my office window I could see them digging the foundations of the new Institute of Pathology. All the growth and new equipment which was on its way kept morale at a high level.

We looked after civilian patients, on a "space available" basis, as well as servicemen and women. It broadened the range of patients we saw and kept up my medical and nursing staff's wider knowledge and skills. Wroughton was very popular with the local population. From time to time, when I was out on the cocktail party circuit, someone meeting me for the first time would say how much they liked the hospital. I always asked them why. There were all sorts of reasons, of course, but three cropped up time and again. Firstly, the nursing sisters wore proper hats. They did indeed wear what were officially known as "veils", but that was nothing to do with me. I had no input whatever into the dress regulations for the Princess Mary's Royal Air Force Nursing Service. Secondly, the staff they saw walking around the hospital always seemed to be happy and were smiling. I probably could claim some credit for that. If my staff were happy, I probably wasn't doing too bad a job.

The third reason people commonly gave was that the main hospital entrance area was always spotlessly clean, with a shiny floor. This was down to a cleaning lady called Winnie. I think today she would be described as having Special Educational Needs, but she knew how to keep a floor clean and took great pride in her work. She defended it too – woe betide anyone she caught making her floor dirty. One morning I had gone to the main entrance to escort a Very Senior Officer who was coming for an outpatient appointment. It was a typical Wroughton wet and windy day and, as I hurried him in, he didn't have time to clean his shoes properly on the mat. He was leaving marks on the floor. Winnie spotted them and came towards us. I attempted unsuccessfully to intervene, but to his great credit the Very Senior Officer apologised to her, walked back to the mat and wiped his feet properly. It was a useful reminder to me that we all contribute in our way to the success of a large enterprise. Winnie, whatever her limitations, played a significant part in people thinking well of my hospital — and by extension, of me.

Not long after I arrived at Wroughton a cloud appeared on the horizon. Despite the very recent downsizing in which I had been involved in my previous job, the defence budget was to be cut still further. A number of Defence Cost Studies were set up, to look at ways of saving more money. Defence Costs Study 15, a phrase which was to haunt me for the rest of my RAF career, was concerned with the medical services. Rumours abounded as to what "DCS 15", as it became known, was trying to do. A reduction in the number of hospitals across the armed forces seemed likely. I was fairly confident about Wroughton to begin with — we were located in central Southern England and had good land communications via the M4 and the main line railway; we were ideally situated for receiving casualties aeromedically evacuated from overseas to Lyneham and Brize Norton; we were near a number of RAF stations and the large army garrison at Tidworth; we had an MRI scanner and modern theatres and were beginning to upgrade other areas; we had lots of room to expand; and if push really came to shove we could even have C130 Hercules aircraft bringing casualties in to the runway at Wroughton airfield itself.

The study team visited us and we presented our case to them. It went very well. We had one rather amusing hiccup. Because I could rapidly close access to the station and provide armed guards in the shape of my RAF policemen, one of the hospital's roles was to provide a secure medical facility for the treatment of VIPs or "high value targets" who might be the subject of terrorist attacks. The Prince of Wales was not far away at Highgrove, the Princess Royal was nearby at Gatcombe Park, and there were a number of other people in the area who fell into the category. I described us as being a "secure hospital". One of the study team was a retired senior civil servant from the Home Office. He looked puzzled, and asked me to go over the point again. Then we both realised what the problem was. While at the Home Office, he had been responsible for running Broadmoor, the high-security psychiatric hospital. To him, a secure hospital was one you couldn't get out of; to me, it was one you couldn't get into.

The results of DCS 15 were to be announced in the House of Commons by the Secretary of State for Defence. I had been given an embargoed copy of the report so that I could prepare a tannoy broadcast to the men and women under my command. The Secretary of State began his statement before the end of the embargo; many of my people were listening to him on the radio. My carefully prepared message was undermined from the start. In brief, all save one of the armed forces hospitals were to close. The NHS would be responsible for the hospital care of service personnel in peacetime (how this was to be achieved given the existing overstretch in the NHS was never explained). The one hospital to remain open would be the Royal Navy Hospital at Haslar, in Gosport. It was housed in buildings dating back to the Napoleonic wars, was in the very south of the country, accessible only through the densely populated Gosport peninsula, and had a final access road that crossed a single-track bridge controlled by traffic lights. Those hospital personnel in the three services who remained would be employed either at Haslar, or at three Ministry of Defence Hospital Units (MDHUs) at Frimley Park in Surrey, Derriford in Devon and Peterborough in Cambridgeshire, but there would be a lot of redundancies. There would of course be savings: that was what it was all about. The usual pinch of salt with which all government figures must be taken disappears into insignificance with the fact that the Wroughton site, valued at £27 million in the DCS report, finally sold for about a sixth of that.

My job had suddenly changed from "oversee the expansion" to "close the hospital by the end of next year". And of course I had to try to maintain morale as well. I was not helped by the system. The edition of the weekly *Royal Air Force News* – the service house magazine – immediately following the announcement of all the reports carried as its front-page headline "Eliminate the Unnecessary to Keep the Essential". I passed one of my Warrant Officers in the corridor the day the *RAF News* came out. He waved his copy at me. "So we're unnecessary, are we sir?" he said. There was no answer to that. I phoned the RAF's Director of Public Relations to complain, but it was too late. The damage had been done.

It was all rather hard, but after twenty-seven years I was imbued with the services' "can do" attitude. I remembered that, many years previously, I had been moaning to Flight Sergeant Nicholson, the Senior NCO Medical Assistant at Bruggen, about some aspect of service life which was irritating me. "Sir," he said, "if you didn't want to be buggered about, you shouldn't have joined." Wise words. Life had to go on, and I had an RAF station to run.

The fighting in the former Yugoslavia and our involvement in it was taking up an increasing amount of our resources. I regularly had to provide surgeons and support staff to man the various surgical support teams in country. The surgeons didn't like going there. There were very few casualties. While this was a good thing overall it meant that they spent their detachment in effect doing nothing. All one of my surgeons did over his three months was remove an ingrowing toenail and carry out a vasectomy on his Flight Sergeant. It was demotivating, and they were rightly worried about losing their skill-of-hand.

It wasn't the same for the support staff – nurses and medical assistants. They tended to be given more responsibility in the field, and many of them enjoyed the stimulation of it all. I had one particular Special Field Nurse – we'll call him Sergeant X – who possessed excellent professional abilities and who, along with his wife, played a full part in the wider activities and needs of the station. His wife was known to be a source of advice and comfort to younger, less experienced airmen's wives, and she was on the Wives' Club committee. He had volunteered for a couple of detachments to the former Yugoslavia, and had been picked on both occasions because he was known to be thoroughly competent and good to work with. Shortly after he had volunteered for a third time, Vivien was telling me over supper about a Wives' Club meeting she had held that afternoon. After it, she told me, Mrs X had mentioned to her what seemed to be unfair treatment of her husband by the system, with him being sent on detachment more often than others of his group. Her complaining to Vivien in that way was completely unacceptable behaviour – an NCO's wife abusing her access to the Commanding Officer's wife in effect to complain about how I was doing my job. The next day I sent for Sergeant X.

Sergeants don't get summoned in front of the Station Commander unless it's fairly important, whether good or bad. Sergeant X didn't know which it was and looked rather anxious as he stood to attention in front of me.

"Sergeant, your wife has abused her position on the Wives' Club committee to complain to my wife that I send you on too many detachments."

Sergeant X went red, then white. "Sorry, sir, I'll..."

"Be quiet. You know as well as I do that what she told my wife isn't quite the whole truth. You have until tomorrow night to tell your wife exactly what happened. If you haven't done so by then, I shall invite her here and I will explain how you came to be sent on the detachments."

"Er, yes, sir. Er..."

I "relented" and smiled at him. "And you do an excellent job. We all know that, and that's why you get picked when you volunteer. Thank you."

"Oh. Thank you, sir." He saluted and left.

I don't know how the conversation between Sergeant X and his wife went, but the next day he contacted the personnel office and withdrew his offer to volunteer for a third time. And of course he was never sent compulsorily, because he had already done more than his fair share. It was a refreshingly good problem to have had to deal with.

The local civilian population was up in arms at the announcement of Wroughton's closure. A "Save Wroughton" campaign was formed, and among other things they planned a protest march from the centre of Swindon to the hospital. The police officer in charge of the arrangements to escort the march contacted my OC General Duties Flight, Flying Officer Bob Wooley, who among other things commanded my RAF Police section, to discuss the march's arrival at the hospital. The main gate was off a narrow, winding country lane, and the policeman felt it would be better if, rather than mill around outside the main gate, the marchers could come in and rally on the rugby pitch just inside it.

Obviously I could not allow this. The armed forces must always be and be seen to be completely apart from politics. I couldn't be involved with a group complaining about government policy. "But," I said to Bob, "if when they arrive the police are worried about the physical safety of the marchers, and fear that someone might be injured, clearly that would be a factor I would have to consider." Bob passed my refusal, and my comments, to the police. The march set out at twelve noon the following Saturday. At about 1201 the duty police Inspector phoned Bob to say that, with crowds on the narrow road and the current level of traffic, he was worried that someone could be injured while they were demonstrating outside our main gate. Could we help? The marchers came on to the rugby pitch and tied their banners to the goalposts. Of course I had to notify my command headquarters about what had happened, but I didn't actually get round to it until the protesters had gone.

It wasn't all doom and gloom; there were a few things to cheer me up. Since coming back from the USA I had become more involved with the Faculty of Occupational Medicine, and was appointed an examiner in 1992. One of my fellow examiners was Dr Eoin Hodgson, who was Director of Occupational Medicine at Oxford University. He was about to go into hospital briefly for a minor operation, and asked if I would cover the Oxford department for a couple of weeks. All I had to do was one clinical session per week and be available for consultation by phone. I managed to persuade my command headquarters that I should be allowed to do it, partly because it would give me some Continuing Professional Development for which the RAF wouldn't have to pay and of course Oxford University is a fairly prestigious place. Any doctor will tell you that, when a doctor becomes a patient, everything that can go wrong will; so it was with Eoin. In the end he was off for eight weeks. It was sometimes quite hard work keeping up with the demands of the station and looking after Oxford, but it was interesting and different work, and it stood me in good stead later.

My increased involvement with the Faculty had obviously been noticed, because one day a letter arrived telling me that I had been elected a Fellow. This was a very reassuring sign that my professional colleagues recognised my worth and when, a few years later, I was elected a Fellow of the Royal Aeronautical Society, I felt that both professions in which I had spent my working life, medicine and aeronautics, had recognised that I'd been there and done my bit. We went up to the Royal College of Physicians for the presentation of my Fellowship Diploma and the celebratory dinner. The day was particularly happy because the Dean of the Faculty at the time was Professor Ewan MacDonald, an old friend who had been best man at our wedding.

The Station Warrant Officer – "the SWO" (pronounced swoh) – is a pivotal post on any RAF station. His job is to maintain what the Air Force Act calls "good order and air force discipline". He is an imposing man of upright bearing and awesome countenance, and he carries with him his badge of office, a large swagger stick topped with the Royal Crest. If he hoves into view and young airmen – even innocent ones – are not put into a state of fear and alarm, he is not doing his job properly. The RAF had just appointed the first ever female SWO. I met her in a corridor of the command headquarters when I was visiting one day. I had vaguely known her on a previous station, when she was a sergeant. She was a trim, well-preserved lady in her early forties; in her starched shirt, tailored skirt, black patent leather court shoes and carrying her swagger stick, she looked rather fine. I congratulated her on her appointment, and asked how it was going. "No problem at all, sir," she replied. "When I approach, the average young airman struggles to work out whether I'm the SWO, his mother, or his domination fantasy come to life. Whichever it is, he does what he's told."

Wroughton hosted the last ever RAF Medical Units Rugby Sevens competition – always a big social event for the medical services and one with lots of rivalry between teams. Wroughton won – a great morale booster for us. The one tiny cloud over it all was that when our captain, Flight Lieutenant Sean McFetridge, my catering officer, accepted the trophy, he said it was the happiest day of his life. The look on his wife's face showed that she felt that that description should perhaps have been kept for something else.

That the defence medical services, and especially the hospital-based part of them, were very unhappy with the outcome of DCS 15 percolated upwards through the organisation. There was no possibility of anything being reversed, of course – all the expected savings had already been incorporated into future budgets – but people at the top felt they should do what they could to manage the situation. I was told that the Chief of the Air Staff (CAS), Air Chief Marshal Sir Michael Graydon, would visit Wroughton to discuss the situation with my medical officers. This was quite literally unprecedented. As far as we could ascertain, no CAS had ever made an official visit to an RAF hospital.

Details of the visit were arranged between me and CAS' personal staff officer (PSO). CAS would arrive mid-morning, give a presentation followed by a question and answer session in the station conference room, then join us for further informal discussions in the mess over lunch. Lady Graydon would accompany him. I arranged that, as he came through the front gates, he would be met by an RAF Police Land Rover, which would escort him to the entrance to Station Headquarters. This was cited as "ceremonial", acknowledging CAS' very senior status. There was another reason for the escort. If it was there, CAS couldn't, immediately after entering the station, go down a side road, stop at some anonymous building, go in and start talking to the unprepared inhabitants in an attempt to get a feeling for the true state of the station. This had been done in the past; all station commanders were aware of it and were keen that it shouldn't happen to them.

We awaited his arrival at Station headquarters. There were chalk marks on the road to show where CAS' car should draw up, and there were two smart young airmen, in best blue and white belts and gloves, to act as door openers. They had been briefed to within an inch of their lives by the SWO, who stood with his eagle eye on them. When the car drew up, the door opener on the near side of the car, who was expecting to be opening the door to CAS, looked in to see a black Labrador. This was Blackie, CAS' dog. The young airman looked up to me with a mixture of panic and dismay on his face. I nodded to him to move forward, where CAS was in the front passenger seat. Lady Graydon was where we were expecting her.

After a short discussion about the best place for his driver to walk Blackie, CAS came in and the visit started. I thought my medical officers were very well behaved under the circumstances. While they didn't take any prisoners, they never became disrespectful or offensive. The lunch went well – Vivien joined us to make the point that all this was very hard on the wives.

A couple of days later I had a letter from the PSO. After the thanks for what we had provided, he went on to say that CAS thought that my medical officers were making things seem worse than they actually were, and that they should put more effort into seeing the opportunities which the new arrangements would give them. I replied saying that if, as a pilot, he were to find his career prospects limited to serving either on a tri-service base at the Army Air Corps Centre at Middle Wallop or else on a detached flight at a small civil airport, he probably wouldn't be very happy, and would have a bit of a struggle to see any opportunities. I knew, of course, that my letter would be seen by CAS, so as soon as it went off I phoned the DG – by this time John Baird, now an Air Vice-Marshal – to tell him what I'd done and warn him about the likely explosion coming his way.

In fact, there was no explosion. Some years later, sitting next to Sir Michael at a dinner, he recalled to the incident, and admitted of DCS 15 that "we took our eyes off the ball with that one".

That summer, for the final Officers' Mess Ball, we chose as a somewhat ironic theme the last voyage of RMS Titanic. The mess was decorated to look suitably nautical and we were piped aboard by a couple of seamen from the naval unit. Just before midnight, at the time Titanic struck the iceberg, everything stopped and we went outside to watch a firework display representing the distress rockets which had been sent up in 1912. It was a dramatic, and also poignant, occasion.

Details were emerging of the future shape of the defence hospital services. They were all to be absorbed into a government agency, which was eventually called the Defence Secondary Care Agency. A number of working parties were set up to work out the nitty-gritty of how it would all happen. I was a member of one of them, which dealt with the organisational structure and manning needs. The role of the Agency would be to train medical personnel so that they would be appropriately qualified and experienced to be deployed in support of the fighting arms in case of conflict. The Chief Executive of the Agency was to be a civilian, probably someone who had experience of running an NHS Trust. The NHS was held up to us as an exemplar of how to run hospitals. I forbore commenting on that.

The deputy to the Chief Executive would be a one-star officer (Commodore/Brigadier/ Air Commodore). He or she would be the Director of Plans and Personnel and would be the senior military officer in the organisation. (S)he would be responsible for providing to the fighting arms such medical support as they required. At one of the working party meetings I suggested that (s)he might have a hard time doing that, as the people concerned would still be controlled by their single service personnel branches. I got from the chairman the sort of look I was getting used to.

Not long after the original announcement of the cuts, details of the redundancy scheme had been announced. The terms were generous. People who fell into the categories where there were to be redundancies were invited to volunteer, in the hope that as few compulsory redundancies as possible would be necessary. Inevitably it caused a good deal of anxiety among my staff. Vivien was active in making sure that the wives had proper support; on more than one occasion she found herself consoling a distraught airman's wife over a cup of coffee in our kitchen. For most people, even with a generous redundancy settlement, the future would be uncertain. In many ways my bigger worries were not for the medical professionals, most of whom were highly attractive to likely future employers, but rather for support staff, such as drivers, RAF policemen and clerks. And of course all the locally employed civilian staff – such as Winnie the cleaner – would lose their jobs.

On the day before the redundancy announcements were to be made I received a number of boxes filled with the redundancy notices and supplementary material. I had decided that the officers commanding the three wings – Wing Commander Kim Daniels, OC Medical Wing (chief doctor), Wing Commander Annie Welford, Matron (no one ever called her OC Nursing Wing) and Wing Commander Andy Green, OC Administrative Wing (adjutant and facilities manager) – would deal with those who had volunteered for redundancy in each of their wings. I would deal with the compulsory redundancies. Kim and Andy had volunteered for redundancy themselves, and had been granted it. Annie was in the zone for redundancy, but didn't want it. I was delighted for her when she was not selected. I broke the embargo to tell them all that they had got what they wanted.

The next day was one of the most unpleasant of my working life. About one third of my staff was made redundant. There is a limit to how many grown men you can have in tears in your office before, even though it's really nothing to do with you, you feel an absolute shit. But eventually it was all done, and the very efficient RAF support system began to swing in to action to help those who were to leave. By late afternoon I was exhausted. At about 1645 my PA buzzed to say that the Pathology Technician Warrant Officer would like to see me. In our hierarchical system, under normal circumstances any problems the Pathology Technician Warrant Officer had should have been dealt with by his consultant; failing that, by OC Medical Wing. But these were not normal circumstances. I asked for him to be sent in.

He came in holding some papers, including a copy of the notice announcing details of the redundancy scheme.

"In here, sir, it says that you should try to release people as soon as possible when they have a job to go to. A number of us in the lab have got jobs in the lab at the Equine Hospital at Lambourn," (a town nearby in what was called The Valley of the Racehorse, with many racing stables). "And they would like us to start next week."

"Well, I'm delighted for you, but I still have a hospital to run. I couldn't possibly let you go next week."

"I thought you'd say that, sir, and reckoning that we would all be made redundant anyway, I've been negotiating with the local NHS hospital. They've agreed to provide a service which my consultant says meets his needs, and the cost is actually less than you would be paying us in wages." He offered me some papers.

I had a quick look at them. What he had said seemed to add up. I was very impressed with his initiative.

"Well, I'll have to get OC Admin Wing check this in the morning, but if it is as you say, then we probably can let you go."

Next day Andy Green checked it all through. It was as the Warrant Officer had said, and I was able to let them go at the end of the week. It was at least one happy outcome from an otherwise dreadful day.

I had not been in a redundancy zone. I had been told that, when the hospital closed, I would go back to the MOD in a policy job on the staff of the Surgeon General. It wasn't a bad job, but it would be a bit tame after what I'd been doing. A couple of weeks after the redundancy announcements, John Baird telephoned.

"Iain, your posting's been changed."

I groaned inwardly. What was it now? But then I'd never had any postings changed in the whole of my previous career, and these were tumultuous times. I gritted my teeth.

"Ah. Thank you for letting me know, sir. Where am I going now?"

"You know the Deputy Chief Executive post in the Agency? You're going to that, on promotion to Air Commodore."

Anyone who knows me is aware that I am never short of words. I was then. I went home as soon as I reasonably could to tell Vivien in person. The next day I telephoned Ron Smith, the Agency's Chief Executive Designate. I introduced myself and asked him when he wanted me to start. "As soon as possible," he said.

I set about negotiating with all concerned. I was hardwired into a number of events to mark Wroughton's closure, but apart from that most of the work had been done and Kim Daniels was perfectly capable of overseeing it in my absence. I persuaded the system that I could go to the Agency, thus being promoted – with the various benefits that would bring – on the 16th of October, but that I would also remain as the station commander at Wroughton until the formal closing parade on the 7th of December.

We held a final Guest Night in the Mess. We invited every previous matron and station commander we could locate, many of whom had gone on to higher things, and, despite the circumstances, had a happy evening full of reminiscences.

The rundown and closure of the hospital had gone smoothly. The last patients had left towards the end of November. Things were being packed away and some people were already moving on to their new posts. The aeromedical evacuation personnel moved to Lyneham and the Naval unit made its own arrangements to stay on its existing site.

We hoped that the final parade and Sunset Ceremony would be held on the parade ground, but the Mechanical Transport Hangar was our bad weather backup. Parades inside buildings are never as good, but sometimes needs must when the wind and rain drive. The day of the parade dawned cold and grey. I had asked the weather man at RAF Lyneham for a detailed local forecast. He assessed that it would be cold, with snow in "mid to late afternoon" – he couldn't be more precise than that. The parade was due to start at 1530.

In the morning I met my Wing Commanders and the people who were going to be setting out the equipment for the parade. There was really only one sensible decision; it would have to be held in the hangar. But I wanted it outside, and it was *my* last hurrah. And anyway, if everyone hated me for it, I didn't care. I was leaving forever the next day. I said, "We'll have it outside." They all cheered.

At 1530 the troops marched on, led by the Western Band of the RAF. Speeches were made. I read a valedictory letter from Princess Alexandra, who had given her name to the hospital. I returned our freedom scroll to the Mayor of Swindon for safe keeping in case of our eventual return. Brian Symes and Alan Kearney had arranged a flypast of Hercules and VC10s – although with the lowering clouds we heard them more than saw them. We knew we had sympathy from on high when, as the bugler played the 'Last Post' and the RAF Ensign was lowered for the last time, huge heavy flakes of snow began to fall slowly from the leaden sky. As the parade marched off into the snow and the band played the RAF March Past there weren't too many dry eyes to be seen.

The next day I signed over the entire site to Flying Officer Bob Wooley as the Officer Commanding the rear party, and took the flag off my car.

13

Ad Astra

Vivien's first degree was in English Language and Literature. In Hong Kong she'd volunteered to teach English to some of the Vietnamese boat people and, discovering that she enjoyed teaching, went on to get a job in a language school in Kowloon. While I was at Staff College, she completed a course to gain a formal qualification in TEFL (Teaching English as a Foreign Language). This allowed her to get a TEFL job when we moved to Bushey Heath. Once again, she found she loved being in the classroom but was beginning to find English grammar rather limiting and started to think about further teacher training. When I got home from work one evening she presented me with a plan – or rather a fait accompli. She had been accepted by a local teacher training college and, once Robin had started boarding school that autumn she would spend a year doing a Post Graduate Certificate in Education which would allow her to teach English and Drama.

The transition from officer's wife to student was a dramatic one. As the oldest student by far on the course, she found herself cast in the role of agony aunt to some of the youngsters who poured out their tales of heartache to her. It was good preparation for being a CO's wife. But there were student escapades as well, including a trip to Amsterdam to take part in a student drama festival; I never did hear all about that – probably just as well.

Her first teaching post was at Haberdashers' Aske's School for Girls in Elstree where she spent two years learning her craft and was just beginning to feel confident as a teacher when, of course, my next posting came through. Leaving "Habs" would have been hard were it not for the excitement of moving to America.

Virginia state regulations meant that Vivien couldn't teach full time during our time in Washington; nor, as she said, would she have wanted to with America to explore. Having Robert E Lee High School on her CV made it stand out and helped her get a job when we returned to London. Then came another break while she took on the full-time job of being the station commander's wife at Wroughton.

We had always had an agreement between us that Vivien would be the loyal service wife and camp follower until I had my tour in command. After that I could jolly well fit in with her. But first we needed to buy a house. Our little cottage in Scotland was fine for holidays, but we had to get ourselves out of married quarters and properly into the housing market. Vivien had by now been appointed Head of English at St Mary's, a girls' boarding school in Wantage. We found a house in a pretty village nearby. Vivien would live there and pursue her teaching while I would weekly board during my time in London. After that we'd think about where we might plan to settle permanently.

Joining the Defence Secondary Care Agency – "the Agency" – at the very beginning was exciting in a lot of ways. Large numbers of people had been made redundant, but I had been promoted. Many units were being closed, but we were opening up and growing. We had a lot of hiring to do, and we had to put the Agency's corporate structure in place. At least in theory, we would have more freedom than an MOD-managed organisation to run our affairs. Ron Smith, our energetic Chief Executive, might have come from an NHS Trust, but he had been an RAF Regiment officer for sixteen years and he had a good understanding of the services.

We had a bureaucratic mountain to climb to produce all the documents that were required before the formal launch on our "Vesting Day" – a paper justifying our formation (I did wonder why this was necessary given that we had been given no choice in the matter, but there you go), a launch document, a framework document, a corporate plan for the first year, and so on. Our Aim was defined as "To make available to Commanders in Chief appropriate medically trained secondary care Service personnel, when required, for training, exercises and deployment."

Much of the preliminary work in forming the joint service hospital at Haslar and setting up the MDHUs had been carried out by members of the Defence Medical Services Implementation Team – the DMSIT. I will leave you to work out how their acronym was usually pronounced. It was not complimentary, but then as bearers of what most people in the defence medical services saw as bad news, they were not popular. However, there was a lot of work still to be done, and there was a good deal of expectation management needed in both the service personnel posted to the MDHUs and the NHS trusts who were to receive them. Sorting out accommodation for everyone was a challenge, and at a time of great change the loss of the cohesive service units in which people were used to working and the support which they provided was a particular problem.

We managed to fill the senior posts at the Agency headquarters fairly easily, but getting middle-ranking staff officers was more difficult. The Agency was not the top career choice for most people, and the individual service personnel branches – rightly, in my opinion, given the massive shake-up we had all been through – insisted on sticking to their normal personnel management procedures, particularly with regard to giving appropriate notice for non-operational moves. Furthermore, they were not slow to point out that their servicemen and women, despite being posted to the Agency, still belonged to them, and that I, as the Director of Personnel, could not do with them entirely as I wanted; I had to agree my intentions with them. This was a problem I had raised in the working party I had previously been part of. It was coming back to bite me.

The more sharp-eyed among you will have noticed that the Agency's Aim said nothing about treating patients. This, according to DCS 15, was the responsibility of the NHS. Of course we treated service personnel when and as best as we could, but there were not the resources which had been there previously. This fact was beginning to dawn on the non-medical parts of all three services. The biggest problem was with minor illnesses or injuries which weren't a threat to health, but did get in the way of people carrying out their service duties.

To use the cliché case, a twenty-five-year-old fighter pilot with an ingrowing toenail is not in need of urgent treatment on medical grounds. But if he can't put his flying boot on because of it, we have someone whom we have spent £10 million training unable to fly his £50 million aircraft. If he is taken to the top of the queue for an operation, there is a strong possibility that a grandmother in her seventies will be pushed down the list. The average NHS Trust chief executive does not want to have to defend that to his local newspaper, so we have a problem. (I have nothing against grandmothers in their seventies – I'm married to one. It's just an example.)

This sort of thing was a problem especially for Army recruit training. Lots of recruits suffered minor injuries during their initial training, but in the past prompt treatment from service sources had sorted most of them out and they didn't need to repeat the course or be held in limbo. This wasn't happening any more, and I got lots of complaints about it. In the end some commanders started to pay for private treatment from their unit budgets as it was overall a more cost-effective way of their achieving their aims.

Many people complained to me that we weren't delivering

the treatment service they expected. Time and again I referred them to DCS 15 and pointed out that that was not what we were there for, and more importantly, not what we were resourced for. A further problem was a shortage of manpower even within our reduced establishment. Increasing numbers of medical personnel were looking at what the defence medical services had become and were leaving as soon as they could. As the Strategic Defence Review of 1998 put it, "The first years of operation of the DSCA were characterised by inadequate resources." It noted that we had only 1300 military medical personnel out of a requirement for 1700 and that "The rhetoric of DMS restructuring has so far outstripped its reality."

I even had a gentle moan from the Assistant Chief of Staff of one of the Services. I reminded him quite sharply that nothing in the situation was of my making, and that it was he, as a member of the Service Board, who had signed up to the new arrangements.

We had overseas commitments as well. Cyprus was fine. John Baird and I had an enjoyable trip out there for a ceremony in which he formally handed over The Princess Mary's RAF Hospital to me, representing the Agency. Gibraltar wasn't fine. We hadn't been able to get an agreement to provide medical care to our standards from the local civilian hospital, and the Royal Navy hospital there was literally falling down. While I was in Gibraltar on a visit to deal with some personnel problems, a large chunk of masonry fell off one of the walls. Fortunately, it was caught by the chicken wire in which the building was swathed against just such an eventuality.

It was all far from satisfactory, but any time I visited our units, I had to put a brave face on it and keep telling our people that everything in the garden was lovely. They knew it wasn't, I knew it wasn't and increasingly I felt that they knew I knew it wasn't. You can only do that for so long. A couple of years later I crossed swords with John Baird, by then the Surgeon General, in the letters page of *The Times*, about what needed to be done to sort out the defence medical services. I described them as having been "totally demoralised" by DCS 15. I think that sums it up best.

We all worked hard to try to make what we had been landed with work. My "can do" attitude was still just about extant, but as time passed it became increasingly apparent to me that it wasn't going to work as things were, and that lots needed to change. I wasn't the only one to think that, but there wasn't going to be any more money available, and sorting it all out was going to take several years.

None of this was making me happy. When we were in America the film *Bull Durham* had become a family favourite. We had a recording of it and watched it many times. Some of the phrases from it had entered our family idiolect. One of them, spoken by Kevin Costner's character in the film, struck me as appropriate to my situation: "This is hopeless; this is utterly f***in' hopeless." I translated it into dog-Latin as "*Sine spe: totam copulansque sine spe*" and put it on the screensaver of my computer. Only one person ever rumbled it; he agreed with me. Vivien complained that, every Friday evening when she picked me up from the station, I was grumpy.

For most of my career in the RAF, my ultimate ambition had been "to become the DG". My recent promotion had put me on a good course to achieve that. But now I wasn't sure that I did want the job, or even that the job would still be available. Nor was I sure that I wanted to spend the last years of my working life sorting out a mess which was not only not of my making, but which I had argued and advised against. Most importantly, it wasn't fun any more. In the middle of 1996 I started to look for another job.

In the British Medical Journal I saw advertised a vacancy for an occupational physician in the John Lewis Partnership, to be the Chief Medical Advisor for Waitrose, their food group. The vacancy had arisen because of the impending retirement of Mickey Venn, who was a former Air Commodore in the RAF Medical Branch. We knew each other well, and I phoned him to ask if he thought I might like the job. He said he thought I would, and even offered to put in a good word for me if I applied. I don't know what, if anything, Mickey did, but after the usual round of interviews, assessments and visits, I got the job.

I put in my papers to leave the RAF. Technically I was applying for Premature Voluntary Release. I had just turned fifty, so I was guaranteed to be released six months after my application, and my pension wouldn't suffer. I would have one month's terminal leave, one month's resettlement period, and I had saved a month's annual leave as part of my plans to go; so I would leave the Agency in three months' time. As soon as I had put the application in my out tray, I took a copy to Ron Smith so that he would be the first to know. He was remarkably civilised about it.

I was dined out of the Service at the first Defence Secondary Care Agency Guest Night, held in the RAMC Headquarters Mess at Millbank. My fellow directors gave me an excellent lunch during my last week in the office, and one Friday afternoon in early January1997 I walked out of the Agency headquarters for the last time. And that was that.

Well, not quite. Vivien had suggested that, as part of my resettlement, I should take myself off for a few days to think about what was a dramatic change in my life. I decided to go on a tour of Places Which Were Important In My Life (note the capitals). I went to Cranwell, where I had taken off on my first solo flight in 1965, drove past the house where Vivien and I had begun our married life, and called in at my first ever consulting room. I went north through St Boswells, the village in the Scottish borders where I had grown up, and the grounds of Fettes in Edinburgh, to Scone in Perthshire. The airfield there, where my University Air Squadron had been based when I first joined, had just been sold, and was closed. A lone Cessna sat on the apron, looking very forlorn.

I crossed over to Glasgow, visited the University and drove past the University Air Squadron town headquarters, where I was delighted to see that there was still a red MG parked outside. Next was Ayr, where I had lived for my first three years, and where a picture of a two-year-old me in an aeroplane on a roundabout had been taken in 1948. I went on to Valley; as I walked in to the medical centre there the civilian nurse who I had appointed twenty years previously looked up and said "Oh, hallo" as though I had just walked out the day before.

On the way home I was going to night stop with John and Kate Garnons Williams in Shrewsbury, but first, in the afternoon I went to RAF Cosford. John was still flying with the Air Experience Flight, but it had moved to Cosford and they now flew Bulldogs. He had managed to wangle an hour's flying for me. I went into their crew room, got into my flying suit and started to get ready. Then one of the aircraft went unserviceable, the programme was shuffled round a bit, and our flight was put back for an hour and a half.

John suggested that we should go to the RAF museum at Cosford – it was only a couple of hundred yards away and people in uniform got in free. After we'd been there for about five minutes, I was aware of a man whom I took to be the manager standing beside me. He said, "Welcome to the museum, sir. Is there anything you would particularly like to do or see?" I was about to look round to see who he was talking to when I realised that it was me. I had almost forgotten that I was still disguised as an Air Commodore. He probably didn't get many of them in his museum on a midweek afternoon. I told him that there was; I would love to see inside the cockpit of the TSR-2 – they had one of the only two remaining specimens of that ill-fated aircraft. A man appeared with a ladder, and we climbed up, opened the cockpit and had a good look round. To this bit of good luck was added some humour. John had morphed into Aide-de-Camp mode, and was holding things, hovering and making obsequious comments. He was very good at it and it was hard not to giggle. We had a fascinating half hour climbing round, into, over and under all sorts of aircraft, then, after thanking the manager, went back to the flight line.

We took off and had a very happy hour's flying; two ageing pilots bimbling about the sky over Shropshire and doing a bit of this and that. We landed at dusk, and by the time we had taxied in, late afternoon had become evening. It was a very fitting ending to it all.

Envoi

Joining the John Lewis Partnership was a very gentle easing into civilian life. The Managing Director of Waitrose, David Felwick, was a former Wing Commander whom I had first met at Staff College when we were both members of the Army Staff College shoot. His number two, the Director of Selling and Marketing, was Alistair McKay, an ex-fighter pilot who as a Group Captain had been the station commander at RAF Wildenrath. The Distribution Director was a former Colonel from the Royal Artillery, and one of the buyers had been a Hussar. The Head of Transport for the Partnership was a Colonel from the Royal Logistic Corps. They were all very welcoming, and it was good to be working for an organisation that was growing rather than constantly being cut.

After a few years the opportunity arose to for me to join Health Management Ltd, an independent occupational medicine provider, as their Medical Director for London. My practice was based in a very swish set of rooms in Harley Street. Our waiting room, looking like a Victorian stuffed parlour, full of furniture with chintz covers, had a grand piano in it. My name was on a brass plate on the door. As a finale to my medical career it absolutely fitted the definition of "Self-Actualisation" described by Maslow in his hierarchy of needs about which I had learned at Farnborough thirty years before.

Vivien and I settled in the pretty village in Oxfordshire. I spent fifteen years as a Magistrate in Oxford, dispensing justice amid the dreaming spires.

But that, as someone once said, is another story.